19/05/2019
BECOMING HIM

Dear Judith

I hope you enjoy Becoming Him.

Lots of love

Landa

First published by MFBooks Joburg, an imprint of Jacana Media
(Pty) Ltd, in 2018

10 Orange Street
Sunnyside
Auckland Park 2092
South Africa
+2711 628 3200
www.jacana.co.za

ISBN 978-1-928420-22-4

Cover design by publicide
Publisher and editor: Melinda Ferguson
Editing by Sean Fraser
Proofreading by Megan Mance
Set in Sabon 11/15pt
Job no. 003341

Printed by **novus print**, a Novus Holdings company

See a complete list of MFBooks Joburg titles at www.jacana.co.za

BECOMING HIM

A Trans Memoir of Triumph

Landa Mabenge

To those who have been denied their truths by a world that dictates who and what they ought to be. To the beautiful beings that exist beyond the social definitions of gender and identity.

May you all journey into becoming the butterflies you are meant to be.

Contents

Prologue

My first memory of feeling like I was a boy is when I am only seven years old. I feel a weird excitement every time I am near my younger cousin, Minky. We grow up side by side, and between feeding chickens and ducks and watering our grandmother's ever-thirsty garden, we play children's games, which almost always include playing 'house-house'. I am permanently glued to her shadow, always insisting that she be 'mother', while I frolic around with my shirt unbuttoned playing 'father'. I feel genuine affection for her. She is also extremely beautiful.

Besides my Minky, I am surrounded by an array of other cousins, both older and younger than me, jampacked into a modest three-bedroomed home in Ncambedlana, a few kilometres outside Mthatha (previously Umtata), the capital of the former Transkei Bantustan. The house is nestled on a slightly slanted plain, overlooking the capital.

At any given point there are at least nine of us at home, making my grandmother's task of taking care of us a full-time job. We grow up calling our grandmother Miss K, a pet name she acquired during her younger days as a schoolteacher.

With such a full house it's inevitable that the cousins get to share beds, and I get to share with my beautiful cousin Minky. I use any opportunity when bedtime comes to cuddle up to her, and kiss her goodnight – a practice I have picked up from *Dallas* and *The Days of our Lives*. Although Miss K has made it clear that no grandchild is allowed to watch age-inappropriate television, I find myself glued to the screen whenever the opportunity arises, lost in Hope and Bo's long and passionate kisses.

I grow up thinking the woman I call "Ma", the woman with whom I share a special bond, is my mother. On a cruel overcast day, when I am ten years old, I discover that Ma is not the mother I have grown up believing she is. But even more shocking is my discovery, two years later when I start to bleed for the first time, that I am the girl I have been told I am, not the boy I know I am.

ONE

Home

I love my Ma with all my heart, even though she dresses me up in rather glamorous dresses with lace bibs and elegant shoes with round toes and little buckles. I don't like them. My favourite shoes are a pair of yellow Elefante open-toe sandals identical to the sandals my boy cousins wear.

As I get older, Ma and I argue a lot over the types of clothes deemed acceptable for a young girl. I simply refuse to wear dresses, insisting rather on long pants and shorts for all occasions.

I begin my schooling at the age of six at Vela Private School, situated in Thornhill, on the outskirts of Umtata, a significant drive from my home in Ncambedlana. But school has rules. I plead with Ma, often with tears streaming down my face, to allow me to wear the summer blue shorts and winter grey pants uniform like all the other boys, but I am always called to order and reminded that I am not a boy, but a girl. I don't believe her. When Ma insists on buying me Barbie dolls, I dismember them, leaving legs, arms and torsos strewn around the yard, while I long for toy guns and cars.

My grandparents, who also live in the house with me and Ma and the cousins, are both teachers, although my grandmother left the profession after she married in 1947. They are both very clever. Miss K loved studying and obtained a diploma in teaching from Dohne College in the small town of Stutterheim. A long time ago, against all odds, my grandfather obtained his Bachelor's degree in the Arts, majoring in English, Xhosa and Latin and an Honours Degree in English. I love listening to him telling me how they met as young teachers at a convention in Port Elizabeth, where they were both teaching.

"I was drawn by her lovely eyes, which she batted almost instinctively, whenever I tried to get an audience with her."

A year after meeting they were married, he was offered principalship at a high school in a small village called Rode, on the outskirts of Mount Ayliff, and it was decided that Miss K would became a housewife and homemaker, while he built his career in education and became the provider. When his tenure was done at Rode High School in 1966, he accepted an opportunity to move his family to Umtata, where he eventually became a schools inspector, under Prime Minister KD Matanzima's government in Transkei.

Each morning homely smells greet me when I awake. My grandmother is an expert coffee brewer, and always has a pot of Mona on the stove, ready to kick-start our day. This is accompanied by fresh oven-baked bread, and on weekends heavenly made roosterbrood.

Besides being a homemaker, my grandmother has an undeniable passion for music, and ensures that all of her children and grandchildren are exposed to and influenced by it. Whenever an opportunity arises, we break into song, and she takes it upon herself to train us through note bashing, so that we can follow the music on a score. It is thus through her love for music that I am magnetised by Handel's *Messiah* and Mozart's *Requiem*, which during my early years are Sunday favourites whenever we are ferried to and from church, or taken on lazy afternoon drives with my grandfather.

Then all of a sudden, when I am ten years old, my grandfather goes missing in action. A few days later, not knowing where he could have gone, I learn that he has been admitted to the TB in-patient section of the Umtata General Hospital.

The hospital is a gigantic white building behind a tall barb-wired fence, with security guards manning the entrance. It feels like he is destined to stay there forever. I spend most of my visits perched at the edge of his bed eagerly awaiting whatever gift he might whisk out of his bedside cabinet for me, which is almost always a perfectly ripe, juicy Granny Smith apple.

By now, I am the only grandchild at home, as all my cousins have been returned to their respective parents across the country. Now the sole benefactor of affection, one Sunday morning, on a reprieve from daily chores, I find myself still snuggled up in bed well into the business of the day. I hear voices in the kitchen. Feeling guilty for lazing in bed so long, I peel back my blankets and sheepishly shuffle my way to the kitchen. I walk in to find Ma and my grandmother in heated discussion with a stranger I remember seeing once or twice before. The woman has a round chubby face, dark piercing eyes and a frown cut into her forehead between her bushy eyebrows.

She is highly irate. Her voice clangs like a broken bell.

"When we leave this afternoon, this child is leaving with us. We have already secured a school for her in PE."

Oblivious to the fact that I am in fact the child being referred to, I climb up onto Ma's lap and snuggle into her arms as I watch the heated scene unfold. I smell her comforting skin and rest my head against the nape of her neck as I have always done. But on this grey, cloudy morning she does not return my affection. I turn towards my grandmother, only to catch a hawkish glare from the PE lady.

My Ma is close to tears. "There is no way you can take this child without proper channels. You cannot give a child away and then magically decide that you want her back when it suits you. If you insist that the child's family is after her then you need to ensure that they come and request the child."

But the church bells are ringing. God is calling us to leave the anger in the kitchen and head off to the Sunday service. When we return from church, my lone suitcase is packed to the brim with all my clothes, including my school uniform. I walk into my grandmother's room to find my cousin Minky, who is here on a weekend visit, folding the last of my vests from an untidy pile.

"Who asked you to pack my clothes?"

"Miss K told me to put all your clothes in this suitcase."

I am a thunderstorm of emotion as I storm out of the bedroom into the kitchen in search of my grandmother. The kitchen is empty, but there are voices coming from outside. I find my grandmother in deep conversation with Uncle JS, Ma's younger brother, who stays with his wife and young son on a farm just down the road from us. I plonk my behind on the stoep, forcing myself to wait my turn to speak, to find out why I am packed and ready to leave.

My grandmother's voice is tired and strained. "Please make sure you come back this afternoon as I foresee issues with your older sister and Lolozi."

The angry voice of the Lady from PE bolts through the house from a point unknown: "I can hear what you are saying about me. Ultimately, Lolozi is my child and I can take her with me if I so wish!"

Uncle JS gets into his royal blue Opel Rekord and drives down the narrow driveway, out the gate towards his farm. My head droops heavy in despair and confusion. By now I know that the child they are referring to must be me. My world is beginning to shatter. As my grandmother walks past me into the house, gently, she takes my arm and signals that I should follow her into her bedroom because she needs to talk to me. She closes the door. There's an urgency in her lowered voice as she tells me I need to very quietly and casually walk outside and then run up the driveway to the outside toilet. She instructs me to sit in there with the door closed until someone comes to get me. My eyes are huge. In a conspiratorial whisper I enquire about my packed clothes and whether or not I am going to be forced to leave home. She assures me that I needn't worry, that this is just a tactic to trick the lady from PE, who goes by the name of Nokuzola or Tilili, into believing that I am indeed leaving, but I am going nowhere.

But before I can make my move, the angry Lady from PE storms into the bedroom, cursing and snatching my luggage from the bed. She instructs me to follow her to the car. "We are leaving," she tells me. Now I really want to pee. I follow her outside. Her companion, Bhut Victor, a large burly man with a beard, has pulled his car into the yard and is sitting like a zombie in the driver's seat, eyes fixed on the gate.

The moment my feet step outside the front door, I dash like lightning towards the remote toilet in the far corner of the yard. Just like my grandmother told me. Out of breath, panting like a wild horse, I close the door and hide, placing my foot as a stopper against the wooden door to prevent anyone other than my grandmother from entering. But my escape is short lived. Within moments the door is attacked. The angry Lady from PE screams that I need to come out and get into the car. My mind races. Slowly I open the door under the pretence of heeding her instruction, but the second I am out I bolt left and dash into the empty plot next door. I race through the weed-infested overgrowth, my heart threatening to tumble out my mouth at any given moment. At the edge of the property, I leopard crawl under the razor-wire fence and leap across the road, paying no mind to the possibility of being driven over by a car. When I finally get to the open veld, I stop only to catch my breath and crouch behind the tall grass. And there I stay hidden, not moving, hardly breathing lest anyone find me.

From where I hide, I see Uncle JS return in his Opel. From behind the long grass, I watch as he parks his vehicle behind the PE car, which is now standing outside the yard. He gallops up the driveway. Seconds later, I see Uncle JS – along with his older brother and Minky's father, Uncle VS – half wrestling, half carrying the screaming Lady from PE towards her car where her zombie husband still waits inside. I watch as she is loaded into the front passenger seat. From my hiding place I see how Uncle VS sternly points them away from the house, in the direction of the capital.

As the silver PE car slowly pulls away my body dissolves into relief but my heart still races. I stay frozen in the veld. My safe world has been shattered. I no longer trust who else will emerge to remove me to places unknown.

Dusk settles and with it a cool summer breeze. I begin to shiver as the cold evening air closes in on me. After what feels like a lifetime, Aunt PP – Ma and Uncle JS's younger sister – waltzes out of the yard calling my name. I stand up slowly and respond with caution: "I am here."

"You can come back now; we need to leave for the hospital."

"No, I'm staying here. What if she comes back to get me?"

No amount of reassuring that the Lady from PE has indeed left convinces me, or coaxes me out of my secret spot. I have seen something terrible and sinister. Aunt PP walks across the street towards my hiding place but when she gets close, I run. Soon, however, I grow weary of the cat-and-mouse game, and as the night curtain descends, clothing the world in black, I finally surrender defeat. Together we walk hand in hand towards the house. All is silent. Nobody speaks of what has happened. Instead, I am offered a plate laden with the Sunday meal, now cold. Stuffed full, I am piled into my grandfather's car, driven by Uncle JS, to ferry us to the hospital. I sit in the back next to Miss K, making sure that my hand is firmly glued within hers at all times. I stare at the back of Ma's head as we silently make our way into the darkening night.

We arrive in the hospital parking lot and, lo and behold, the silver car is there. My heart instantly returns to a state of panic. I sink down, willing my chubby ten-year-old body to slip between the folds of the back seats. Perhaps I can make myself invisible in the dark space beneath the front passenger seat. In a hoarse whisper, Miss K instructs me to lock all the doors from the inside as soon as she gets out of the vehicle and implores me to remain out of sight. I do as instructed, braving only a glimpse out of the window to gauge what imminent danger lurks beyond the safety of the locking mechanism. The eyes that meet mine are emblazoned with fury, glinting with a hint of evil. The Lady from PE hammers against the back window with all her might. My grandmother, now outside the car, stands her ground, lashing back and declaring that "this child is going nowhere". The banging on the window continues unabated for what seems like a lifetime. Eventually there is silence.

When the tenuous sense of safety returns, I slowly inch my way out of my crouching position, back onto the seat. I peek out of the window to catch the PE accomplice, Bhut Victor, make his way into the hospital, closely followed by Tando, who I'm told is my brother and who once stayed with us, but has been living for the last few years with the angry Lady from PE, her accomplice and their two young children. From inside the car I watch Ma, Miss K and Uncle JS disappear through the entrance of the hospital, sucked into the cold corridors. A while later, Tando emerges and walks straight towards the silver PE car where he casually opens the boot and removes the suitcase containing all my clothes, stolen from my grandmother's bedroom a few hours earlier. I hazard a sigh of relief; surely this is an indication that my attempted kidnapping is now over.

He walks a few paces between the two vehicles and neatly places my suitcase on the closed boot top of our car. I try to catch a glimpse of his face, if only to thank him for returning my clothes. No eye contact is made. He walks back to the silver car, climbs inside and waits in the backseat with the two small children. From where I am hiding I realise that the Lady from PE is sitting in the front passenger seat. I crouch even lower between the seats. The giant of a man, Bhut Victor, emerges from the hospital, exchanging what seems like pleasantries with Uncle JS. He gets into the silver car, and a few seconds later the car pulls off.

Only when I am absolutely certain that they have truly left, do I unlock the car and slowly get out. I follow my Uncle JS into the hospital. For now the nightmare of the day is shelved as I perch myself on the edge of my grandfather's bed, waiting for whatever he will gift me. As always, he rests against a mountain of white pillows. With a gleam in his eyes he beckons me closer with an affectionate "Sondela mzukulwana wam" (Come closer, my grandchild) and pulls out a sparkling green apple. I devour it. An apple has never tasted this good. Between my crunching I become aware that a dampened mood has descended on the room. All the adults are trying to speak in code around the events that unfolded earlier but I hang onto every word, trying to piece together what little I can. I manage to discover that there is a possibility that I might soon have to move to PE. I work out that the furious Lady from PE is in fact my grandparents' eldest daughter and the zombie, Bhut Victor, who accompanies her, is her husband. I manage to piece together that they have come to demand that I go and live with them and that my grandfather has requested that they give me enough time to finish the current year at school and only begin my transition to them within the following year or two. I search for Ma's eyes but she looks at everyone and everything but me.

At the end of visiting hour, we all bid our goodbyes to my grandfather and return to our car. I stay glued to Ma's hip and insist on sitting on her lap in the front passenger seat as we make our way home into the dark night. It has got much colder.

The minute we get home, eager to continue the adult conversation that has been held in code in my presence at the hospital, I scurry about the house, desperate to complete my Sunday-night chores. I need to speak to Ma; I need to make sense of why it is that I will have to leave the only home I have ever known.

"Ma, am I going to have to leave? Who was that lady and why is she so upset?"

Ma turns her head away from me. She tries to swallow back the tears now welling from her eyes. I move closer; I want to know. I want to know everything. But most of all I want to know why she is willing to give me away to someone so angry, so ugly, someone I barely know. I cup my left arm within her right one and rest my head against her warm chest.

Finally she speaks. Her tone is quiet and sombre.

"I remember the first day I laid my eyes on you. The year was 1981 and I had recently started teaching at Misty Mount. One day I got home to find your grandmother had packed a small overnight bag for me with instructions to go and see my older sister Nokuzola in Port Elizabeth. When I asked her what was wrong, she told me she had received a call that my sister was not feeling well. Your grandmother had decided that I should go and visit Sis Nokuzola so I could assess the situation."

I snuggle in closer to Ma. The closer I get the more I hope I will be able to understand this story. "Your grandfather took me to the bus station – they were called railways back in those days. I bought a ticket and soon was informed by the conductor that the bus was about to leave. I waved your grandfather goodbye. When I got on the bus I showed my ticket to the driver and walked down its dark narrow passage and found a seat close to the back."

This story is taking longer than I thought. I want her to get to the part that is about me.

"I got to PE early the next morning and was picked up from the bus station by Bhut Victor."

"Bhut Victor? Is he the man who was driving the silver car?" I don't dare to say, "Is he the zombie?"

"Yes, that is him; he is my sister's husband. When we got to his home he showed me the outside room he shared with Sis Nokuzola – or Tilili, as we sometimes call her. I was shocked to discover her living with him and his family. I walked into their room to find a baby girl lying on the bed. She was just a few hours old."

I am mesmerised. I sense that I am about to hear something huge. A secret that will change the colour of the sky forever. "It turned out that there was nothing wrong with my sister other than that she had recently had a baby girl and that is why I had to go and see her. I was later introduced to the family she stayed with. They had a lot of questions for me, mostly about where I came from, who my parents were and about what the relationship was between Sis Nokuzola and me as we had different surnames."

I am losing patience now; I need to know more – I need to know much more, but only the parts about *me*. When is this story going to start including my part? But Ma is intent on giving all the boring details. "What I found very strange was the confusion this family had about our different surnames. Sis Nokuzola had been married to the Jekubeni family before, and since I am a Danana, they found that to be extremely amiss. As I was about to explain this to their elderly father, Sis Nokuzola interjected and told them that the reason our surnames differed was because we had different mothers. Our father had been married before and so she had elected to retain her mother's previous surname. This was not true. But I decided to hold my silence."

At last this stuff is getting more interesting. I move from leaning against Ma to crouching on the floor in front of her. I stare straight into her eyes, trying to drink in all this new information. I sense that the great reveal, the grand finale, is looming closer.

"Then we retired to bed for the night. My sister insisted that her baby share a bed with me. The baby had not yet suckled on her breasts, so it was easy to prepare a bottle of formula milk. I was careful as I cradled her in my arms that night. I hardly slept and kept waking up to make sure she was still breathing. Early the next morning I awoke to find my sister frantically packing the baby's clothes into a small bag. She told me to wait in the bedroom until everyone had left for the day."

What I hear next tears my heart into a million shreds.

"That baby was you."

I almost collapse to the floor and sit numb, in a motionless position, until I am jerked back to reality by Ma vigorously shaking my shoulders to make sure I am okay.

The words bang and crash off the walls, bounce and swerve in a bend. They can't seem to find a home in my head. *Who am I who am I who am I?*

I listen dead silent as the next part of the story unfolds. It turns out that overnight the woman I have called Ma all my life now becomes my aunt. After the Mabenges all leave for work, the woman I now learn is my real mother, the ruthless angry soul who threatened to tear me so violently away from my home just a few hours earlier, tells the woman who has been Ma to me all my life that she does not want me. She makes it clear that she is not prepared to raise a child in the conditions she finds herself in. And so, at just two days old, I am given away like a packet of rice by my birth mother to her sister with stern instructions to take me back to Umtata with her.

"She told me she did not want you and I could have you and keep you as my own. She accompanied me to the bus. I carried you in a tiny baby carrier. When we got to the bus station she reminded me that I was never to return you to her. I thanked her and climbed aboard the bus, a new mother. I did not know how I was going to explain you to my father, your grandfather, but I hoped he would understand. We arrived in Umtata that evening, there was an iciness in the air as winter was looming. My father was already waiting for us at the bus station. He looked confused and asked me what I was carrying. I told him I was carrying a child."

Ma pauses for a brief moment, smiling to reveal her beautiful teeth. I can see her as that young woman. Full of love carrying me from that bus. "He asked me whose child this was. I told him, 'This is my child. She was given to me by Sis Nokuzola.'"

I interrupt her. I am a ball of anger and confusion. "If this woman did not want me and gave me to you, then why has she come back now to take me away?'

Ma is at a loss for words.

"It could be pressure from the family she has married into or it could be that she is now in a position to take you back. I do not know, my child."

Before she can continue I flee, run from the bedroom that was once my cocoon. I run. Out of the front door I hurtle. Onto the gigantic veranda. I crawl into a spot beneath the dining-room window and there I pour my heart out. I weep and weep and weep. Bitterly. The fact that I once belonged to someone else does not bother me. The fact that she has come with such arrogance and anger, trying to remove me is not the worst. What hammers at my fragile ten-year-old heart is the loss of a mother – my Ma, who I have known and loved since I first took breath on this earth. That for me is the greatest defeat – that I never belonged to Ma and she never was mine.

TWO

Relocation

Months after the Lady from PE and her zombie husband try to steal me, my grandfather returns home from the hospital. It's 1992. I am now eleven years old and have almost forgotten that nightmarish incident, forcing my mind to wipe it away. His return is a momentous occasion for me. As soon as he is home I flitter around him, faffing and working hard to fulfil his every desire, to ensure that he will never leave again.

We often spend the afternoons nestled in the dining room. Part of his secluded afternoon ritual includes him reading his latest Reader's Digest purchase or frantically typing away on his aged shocking-red typewriter. I enjoy sitting under the table as he hammers away at the tiny keys, providing a rhythmic tune, a welcome absolution from the wireless, blaring Radio Transkei tunes that keep Miss K's foot tapping in the kitchen.

One afternoon I return from school to find my grandfather folding my mid-year Grade 6 report and placing it into an envelope. Driven by curiosity, I ask him what he is doing. He informs me that he is going to post it to PE because I will be starting my schooling there soon. Although I have heard all of this before, it has been a year since the failed attempt at my forced relocation. I have buried this idea far away in the back of my mind. I sigh heavily. I do not want to engage in this conversation. I want to block my ears. I'd much rather spend the remainder of the afternoon playing house outside with my invisible wife and children.

A few months later, Ma and I are summoned to the dining room and advised that we will soon be travelling to PE so that I can take my entrance exam to get into a Model-C school the following year, 1993. I am all too aware of the agony that rises in Ma's usually rosy cheeks. I know she has agreed to the upcoming trip, but I know too that it is eating her up inside. I follow her as she walks down the narrow dimly lit passage into the bedroom we share. We sit for what seems like a lifetime in silence.

"Was the white man who came here last year who asked me all those questions preparing me for this?"

She stays deathly still. No response. I keep nudging her. I desperately need to know what is going on and she is the only person who can provide me with answers.

"No."

We have been reduced to one-word answers. I know I should probably leave the room and allow the waters to settle. Though I know her love for me is unshakeable, I also know the meaning of single-worded responses. Finally, she speaks.

"The white man was from a private school in Grahamstown. I was trying to get you into a better school, but that is not going to happen."

Early one morning a few days later, wordlessly we make our way to town and board a bus for PE. Ma spends most of the journey in a sombre mood, saying only the bare minimum when she makes sure that I am fed and comfortable as we travel along the never-ending road to an unknown destination. With each horizon we reach the knot in my tummy gets harder. Finally we arrive in a much larger town and are met at the station by the passive giant of a man, who I now refer to as the Zombie, who accompanied *her* when she tried to steal me. He greets us hastily and ushers us into his silver car. After a drive in complete silence we arrive at a house perched at the bottom of a slanted hill in a township called kwaMagxaki. It's about eight or nine in the evening. It is dark.

The Lady from PE – or The Mother, as I will soon refer to

her – is waiting for us as we walk through the front door. My entire being is thrown into disarray. There is nothing warm or welcoming about her. She avoids looking at me, and remains seated as we enter the small dining area. Her legs are crossed in front of her, occasionally swaying up and down. Her arms remain folded tightly across her chest. When she speaks, unlike Ma's rich honey voice, hers is high pitched. It cuts like daggers in my ears. I cannot find a single word to say to her.

Seated in the adjacent living room with its bright pink sofas and an aged La-Z-Boy chair are three children, including Tando, the brother I once had. The mother's helper is instructed to show Ma and me to our sleeping quarters and we sheepishly follow her past the dining area and through a door that leads into a narrow passage. To the left is the first bedroom, with a double bunk and a three-quarter bed. Ma and I are to share the bed. We place our belongings on the edge of the bed because there is virtually no room to move. There are no words spoken between us. We walk back into the lounge and sit down on the double sofa. The two youngest children are glued to the TV. One has her thumb firmly locked in her mouth while the other's nose almost touches the screen. I am suddenly aware of deep hunger pangs so I whisper into Ma's ears, but she simply ignores me and carries on speaking to her sister and her zombie husband. Without looking at me, she who is now my new mother instructs me to go assist the helper with the food. Her tone is hard. I don't move. I stay firmly wedged between the armrest and Ma as experience has shown me the brutality that could discharge from this woman at any moment. Perhaps driven by the knowledge of how things could quickly spiral out of control, Ma interjects and announces that she will sort us out herself. But The Mother insists. "She needs to learn her way around the kitchen, so she must do as I have instructed."

I am frozen. I must be "she". Her bark pierces through the layers of my eleven-year-old heart.

Ma leaps to her feet, grabs my hand and walks me to the kitchen without uttering a word. Back home I have never been forced to do any domestic duties save for washing my own vests, socks and underwear. Whenever my grandmother has suggested that I be weaned into the domestics of young girls' duties such as cooking and cleaning, I have interjected strongly and told her I prefer the garden chores.

Now we walk into the miniature kitchen to warm the meal – a concoction of snow-white rice, charred cabbage, potatoes and a skinny drumstick.

I hardly taste a thing, as I gulp it all hungrily down. Soon I have all but polished my plate. Ma and I then rinse the dishes at the tiny, awkwardly placed sink. I can't help but compare every inch of this house to Ncambedlana. Nothing feels normal, nothing feels like home.

With supper and dishes done, Ma and I linger in the tiny kitchen until The Mother retires to bed. Then we make our way to the allotted bedroom. When I eventually fall asleep, I clutch onto Ma as though my life depends on it.

When morning comes I wake with my heart full of fear. Soon we embark on the great trek to Summerwood Primary School in Summerstrand. We are a large contingent: there's Ma, The Mother, as well as the Zombie and their young son, Kaz, my new brother.

Most of the people who surround us are white, with only a few other black parents. The school is massive, the grounds vast – and I fall in love at first sight. There is something safe about it. We shuffle into the school hall where we are instructed on the formalities of the written test. I am introduced to the only other black child who will be testing for the same grade. I am shocked, however, to discover that most of the work seems overly familiar. I have been under the assumption that I am testing for entrance to Grade 7, only to realise that this is a Grade 6 exam. I complete the test quickly.

When it's over we rejoin our families waiting outside. I march straight to Ma and tug on her to move closer. I am aware of The Mother's glare, so I turn to Ma and whisper, "Why have I had to write a test for Grade 6? Why do I need to repeat a grade I am already flying through?"

Ma ignores me. I decide to let this one go. She is not her usual self among these people.

The rest of the day is spent inside the house, mostly in silence. We are due to leave in the morning to return to Umtata. As night falls, I overhear Ma ask The Mother why it is that I have written a test for my current grade instead of Grade 7.

"The school she has been attending is in the Transkei and therefore of a lower standard academically. Her acceptance at the new school will be conditional, and if she passes with stellar marks they will promote her mid-year to the following grade." I later discover that this is all a lie.

The following day we arrive back home in time for evening prayers, after which my grandfather asks Ma to give him the full details of the events that have unfolded in PE.

"Sis Nokuzola says the school was not willing to admit the child for Grade 7 so she will have to repeat Grade 6."

My grandfather is visibly upset.

"That does not make sense. This child always passes with stellar grades!"

As a teacher, he is well aware of the standard of education my current school, Vela Private School, has afforded me and refuses to believe that a state school can disregard the level of a private school, be it in a Bantustan or not. I have learned to mind my grandfather's rage. When on the rare occasion he does raise his voice, I usually disappear and stay well out of sight. As much as I adore him, I know it's best to make myself scarce, to remove myself from the fires of his fury.

O

The rest of the year with Ma and my grandparents flies by too quickly. My final report is sent to PE. I have passed exceptionally well, but instead of being promoted to Grade 7 I will start the year at my new school in PE repeating Grade 6.

It is only years later when sorting through some of The Mother's papers that I come across my Grade 6 report from Vela. I'm astonished to read "promoted to Grade 7", and horrified to see that it has been crudely altered to read "Grade 6". She deliberately changed the grade and forced me to repeat a year I had passed with flying colours. Her entire story had been a lie.

After that discovery, one night in hushed whispers in the house in PE, I discuss the altered report with Tando during one of our discreet evening meetings. He explains that Kaz, The Mother's beloved youngest son, had failed and been forced to repeat a grade before moving to Summerwood. By holding me back a year, there wouldn't be too big a gap between us. The Mother thrives on pitting me against her youngest son who she constantly praises as the one who "is destined for great things", who will "become a physician one day", while I, on the other hand, am continually reminded that I will "never amount to anything", and that I am "doomed to failure".

Long before I am ready to leave my beloved Ma and the only home I have ever known, I am summonsed to PE sooner than expected to prepare for the following academic year. I have no voice or power to resist. I am led like a lamb to the slaughter.

On a sweltering summer's day in early December 1992, Ma and I board a minibus for PE. I have noticed a scratchiness about Ma in the weeks leading up to our departure. She has become snippy, snapping at me for the smallest of things. When I forget to warm her food one evening when she arrives home later than usual, out of nowhere, she slaps me across the face. It is the first time she has ever raised a hand to me. She has even started missing out our mandatory 5:30 evening home prayers.

As we leave the familiar roads of Umtata behind, Ma spends the long journey gazing out of the window. We arrive in PE well into the evening. We are hardly greeted when we enter the house and led to the same room where we last spent the night there together. This time, I am instructed to share the bottom bunk bed with the helper, Lungelwa. I oblige, wordlessly. I know instinctively that I will have no freedom of existence in this house, and I will soon come to realise that any defiance on my part will yield outcomes detrimental to my being.

The next morning at around 7am, I wake to find the three-quarter bed across from me empty. It is neatly made; there is no trace that Ma has ever slept there. My throat closes. My heart beats with suffocating anxiety. Seconds later I hear the front door open and close. I slip out of bed. Barefoot I walk the two steps to the giant window facing the hill we walked up earlier in the year as we navigated our way to the taxi rank. I pull the curtain back and watch as Ma, now reduced to being my aunt, makes her way up the road accompanied by my brother, Tando, carrying her overnight bag in one hand. I want to bang on the window, shout, scream, leap out and chase her down the street and beg her to return or take me with her. But my mouth doesn't move; my nose stays glued to the window. Only my eyes move as they well up with tears. I watch Ma get smaller and smaller until she vanishes into the folds of the horizon. She has left no note and has uttered no goodbye.

THREE

The New House

The first week snails by as I slowly find my place in the new home. Somehow I manage to force myself to adjust my thinking and realise that there is nothing to be done. I must try to get used to it, for nothing else if not my sanity. I am immediately assigned chores, overseen by Tando, who has been instructed to rope me in so I can learn what is expected of me. The outdoors are out of bounds and luxuries such as television or sleeping in on weekends are reserved exclusively for the youngest two children, who are as unwelcoming and detached as The Mother. While Tando and I work tirelessly to keep the house in order, The Parents and their two youngest are a cosy unit, sharing hugs, kisses and affection. Since my relocation, there have been no formal introductions, but I soon learn that the boy, Kaz, is a year younger than me and the girl, Ney, is eight years my junior.

One morning, soon after my arrival, we are piled into the silver car and ferried to Birch's retailers to buy our uniforms for the following school year. It is clearer than ever that there is a definite hierarchy among the inhabitants of this house, with two distinct camps: The Parents and the two youngest kids on one side, and Tando, Lungelwa and me on the other.

On the trip to Birch's, Tando has been left behind at home and I have the rare honour of travelling with The Parents and their beloved children. We arrive at the Birch's store and my heart begins to beam in anticipation. I am eager to forget that I have been abandoned and focus on the fact that I will now be getting a new spread from head to toe. I feel like a toddler in a candy store. Most of the time I maintain composure and act tough, but today I feel like running up and down the aisles. The Parents enquire about the specifics we require and we are ushered to changing rooms and items are brought to us to try on. My heart sinks the minute I am handed a Von Trapp-like Scottish tunic in blue. I glance at the changing room across from me and notice Kaz trying on a pair of grey shorts. I ache to receive the same. In my mind and heart, we are the same gender and I cannot understand why we can't wear the same uniforms, especially since we are more or less similar in age. The look of disappointment on my face betrays me. The Mother shoots daggers at me.

"I will show you flames when we get home," she hisses.

I am terrified, so I scurry back into my cubicle, tail between my legs, and hurriedly pull on the new uniform. I emerge from the cubicle kitted out in the Von Trapp outfit, eyes downcast, awaiting her piercing approval. She merely nods her head and instructs me to change back into my civilian clothes as we have limited time and still need to look for other uniform accessories.

So we move on to swimwear. I cannot help but feel insulted at having to wear a body suit while my younger brother gets neat briefs, but this time I am careful to hide my disdain and not evoke any further fury from The Mother. Although I manage to fake a neutral face, inside I am weeping as I move around the store, agreeing to every item she deems necessary and suitable for me. As we drive back home in the silver car, the atmosphere is gloomy, the sounds of The Crusaders strumming along to the pain I feel. Every fibre of my being yearns to return to Umtata. But it is useless to long for the impossible ...

Back at the house, I trudge through the adjacent garage door into the lounge. The bright red carpet feels like it's scooping me into its hellfire. I move past the pearly white TV cabinet, straight towards the dining room and into the narrow passage to the room

I share with Tando and Lungelwa. I place the packets of girls' clothes in the corner and slump onto the floor, distraught by my own powerlessness.

"Lolozi! Lolozi!"

I am jolted back to reality by her screeching voice summoning me. I am taken aback that she uses a name tinged with affection, my nickname from Umtata. I dash out the room into the kitchen only to be greeted by the kettle electric cord. One lash, two lashes, three. I lose count. I try to cover my face as the cord stings.

"You will never question my authority again! *Thwack*. You will do as I tell you! *Thwack*. You come here from Umtata ill disciplined because those whores who raised you have let you get away with everything! *Thwack. Thwack. Thwack*. Next thing you will be telling me how to run my house."

This is the first time in my life that I get a beating. Harmless hidings have been plenty from Miss K, but this is an improper lashing. As I cower in the corner I can almost pluck the rage from the creases embedded between her eyebrows. Her eyes are on fire. I manage to stumble up and run from her to the lounge, desperate to find a place of safety. I feel a trickle relieving itself from my bladder. I dash towards The Father, the zombie who's been dozing on the La-Z-Boy, the low buzz of the TV in unison with his intermittent snores.

The Mother is hot on my heels. I instinctively leap onto The Father's lap and try to bury my face into the hoped-for safety of his huge chest. She comes charging, electric cord lasso still lashing, her fuse fully ignited, as I beg him to get her to stop. After what seems like an eternity, he mutters, "That's enough, Nokuzola."

His request goes ignored. She continues in a frenzy.

When her rage is finally quenched, she roars, "Hamba apha! Suka phambi kwami! (Go away! Remove yourself from my sight!)

As she leaves, I slowly withdraw from The Father's lap; its safety has failed me. I walk cautiously to the toilet, lest my waters tumble down my legs. As I pass the kitchen, The Mother plugs the kettle cord back into its socket. Triumphantly, she calls out to me, "uVictor akayondoda yakho."

23

I do not understand what this means. I know the name Victor, I know *ndoda* means "man" and I know *akayoyakho* means "is not yours". I stare at the floor and mumble an apology. Perhaps she means Victor is not my father and so cannot be my protector. I can live with that; I have never had a father.

FOUR

Escape

In the mornings I wake at 6am to prepare and pack lunches for everyone. My brother Tando, Lungelwa and I take turns fulfilling domestic duties while the rest of the house sleeps in. I hardly have enough time to process my demotion from an eleven-year-old to domestic worker. Depending on The Mother's mood the night before, there are rare times that she grudgingly permits me to prepare the lunch the previous night, allowing me an extra ten to fifteen minutes of sleep. By 6:45am I have to be done and ready for school, wearing the ridiculous Von Trapp tunic, the source of my electric cord humiliation.

Days turn into weeks but the agony of my displacement lingers. My servant duties continue well into the weekend when I am initiated into the world of hand washing the clothes of the entire family. Over time I become well versed in the art of doing a full week's laundry on a Sunday morning, and depending on what the duty roster for the week looks like, Tando and I alternate washing and ironing.

On Saturdays I am introduced to the local Seventh Day Adventist Church where The Parents are staunch and devoted members. I am assigned to worship with youngsters my age and expected to quickly adjust to the routines of the church. Although I make an effort to understand the underlying doctrines and mandatory pathfinder events, the church refuses to grow on me. I feel displaced as I listen to the repeated teachings about the superiority of this particular faith over others. As a person who has been baptised and was welcomed into the Methodist Church as a baby, I can't bring myself to embrace these harsh doctrines from which I instinctively feel ostracised, despite The Mother strongly suggesting that I am rebaptised into the faith. A lot of the teachings do not make sense to me and, as I grow older and begin to develop an identity and personal understanding about the Church, its foundation and teachings, I choose not to become a committed member. From the outset I am achingly aware of the hypocrisy presented by my "perfect church family" who at home transforms into an abusive and neglectful pack of hyenas.

Each night before I sleep I ache for the love and affection Ma showered on me in the first eleven years of my life. There is none of it for me from The Mother. I am even more bitter as I watch how she exudes love for and lavishes treats on her beloved younger children while Tando and I are treated like slaves. While we are squeezed into the tiny side room, with the help, her precious Kaz sleeps on a mattress next to The Parents' double bed, and Princess Ney gets to snuggle in between them. The third bedroom stands empty, exclusively reserved for Kaz, for some date in the near future should he decide he wants his own room.

One Saturday morning, after enduring my new home for three long months, I wake up early and decide to run away. The Father, who is a paramedic, has already left for his morning shift. The Mother, who is a nurse, is working night shift and will only be home just after 8am. This gives me an hour's window to stuff all I can into one suitcase and a black plastic bag to make my escape. When Ma dropped me off, she stuffed two R20 notes into my hands, whispering that I should hide them. I have carefully stashed the precious notes under the inner soles of my Reebok sneakers, where I sense no one will look. I have also managed to "borrow" a crumpled R10 after rummaging through Lungelwa's belongings. I pray that the taxi back to Umtata will not cost more. I creep out the bedroom clutching my belongings, and make my way out of the back door dressed in my shockingly bright mustard tracksuit pants, a white sweater and sneakers. Although I am not certain of where I am heading, I do remember how to get to the garage where I hope I can board a taxi to the rank and find my way to Umtata from there.

My heart is racing as I hurriedly make my way up the same hill that swallowed Ma just a few months back. Each step is a homage to determination. Once I get to the Engen garage I'm told by a petrol attendant to stand in front and flag down the next taxi, which will be headed for the Njoli rank. Once I am safely in the taxi it seems to take forever, but finally I arrive in a place bustling with vendors and street hawkers selling everything from clothes to mealies to tripe. I frantically walk up and down, aware that The Mother will be home at any minute and is sure to discover me missing. In a state of panic, I try to find the taxi to Umtata. Above each lane hangs a sign indicating the various destinations. Eventually I spot Umtata and make my way to the first vehicle in the queue, hoping the conductor and driver will allow me a boarding pass.

"How old are you and why are you travelling on your own?"

I shake as I respond. "I am almost twelve ... and I was here visiting relatives but now I have to go back home to Umtata. I live there with my grandparents and mother in Ncambedlana."

The conductor scans me from head to toe. He does not seem convinced but agrees to let me board. He hands me a register to fill in and instructs me to fill out the details of where I am going, including a home telephone number. Thankfully, this information has been drilled into me by my previous homeroom teacher. I fill it in perfectly. The conductor informs me that the full fare will be R40 and the heavens sing as I hand him my precious crumpled notes. The taxi fills up very slowly. My hunger pangs whisper through the growling in my stomach. With at least ten people to still go before we fill up, I decide to walk around the vendors parading an assortment of fruits and nibbles in the hope that I can afford some sustenance with the silver coins jingling in the pockets of my sweat pants.

As I walk up and down, my head floating in the clouds, dreaming of the loving reception I will get when I arrive home, I hear the

27

familiar screeching terror-inducing voice, "Bamba loomntana unxibe iblukhwe ethyeli! Mbabeni!" (Grab that child in yellow pants!)

I swing my head back to find her swooping like a huge angry vulture through the bustling crowd. She charges at me, faster and faster, and I turn and run, ducking and diving between the onlookers watching with glee as the drama unfolds. I hurtle past the fruit stalls and before I make my way into the most crowded section of the rank with its bright red Coca-Cola containers, my brother Tando appears to my left. For a second I think he's here to help me escape but he chases after me. Why is he part of this enemy contingent? I can't keep up the pace and then *oomph!* I run straight into a man I have seen only a few times since my arrival in PE. My father's youngest brother grabs me by the scruff of my T-shirt and commands me to stop running. He drags me straight into the arms of The Mother, the vulture who claws me by the nape of my neck and all but squeezes the life out of me.

"Uzawufa fi namhlanje" (You are going to die today). I look up at her, my eyes filled with tears, and beg her forgiveness, knowing well that there will be no mercy.

She drags me towards a strange car, yanks open the back door and bundles me into the empty back seat. The driver, a fair-skinned lady I have never met before, sits motionless behind the wheel. The Mother climbs into the front passenger seat and signals to the driver to leave – Tando will follow with my belongings in my captor's car.

"Uba ucinga ukuba uyathandwa eMtata uyazikhohlisa. Abanaxesha lakho abantu bapha." (If you think they love you in Umtata you are fooling yourself. That family does not care about you.)

I remain as rigid as a rod, scared to even breathe lest that evokes additional wrath. Within no time we arrive home and she banishes me from her sight. Unsure whether to go inside or nestle myself in the outside naughty corner, I choose the latter. The anguish of knowing that I have brought this on myself drives me to a tipping point. Tears flow from my eyes as I wonder what is to become of me. Moments later The Father arrives. He commands me to get up from my crouched position and follow him into the house.

The Father smashes my head against the wall closest to the door. My brain goes numb immediately, followed by a deafening buzzing in my ears. I stumble to the floor. The angry giant lifts me up and throws me against the wall for a second time. This time my head hits the light switch and I flip back, bouncing rhythmically against the doorframe.

Dressed in his paramedic uniform, a white shirt and navy slacks, The Father continues his lashings. As I stagger up, I beg for him to stop, I beg for my life. I try to run. The Mother watches, smiling, perfectly perched on her pink dining chair, feet locked out in front of her, jovially swaying up and down. Arms folded across her chest, she spurs him on. The more I plead for my life, the louder her "Mbethe! Mbetha loosathana" (Beat her! Beat that devil up!) crescendos …

Now The Father's gigantic size-12 foot digs into my ribs. I am crouched on the floor like a beetle, trying to creep into a corner that will provide me with no safety. His face contorts in hatred. His pupils are dilated, the whites of eyes as crisp as the shirt he is wearing, the one I carefully ironed last night. I search for his soul through the raging fires in his eyes. My T-shirt is now splattered with blood. I beg him to stop. He is deaf to my pleas.

I hear her chair chafe against the carpet. Perhaps she is finally coming to pull him from me. If wishes were horses … Instead, she returns and hands him the infamous kettle cord. Now they are a true team. His shoe, her cord. My body is thrashed into a motionlessness ball. There are no screams left. But still he continues, nudging me every now and again to ensure that I am still alive. I wet myself. I am defeated.

When the monster has finally quenched his thirst for revenge I am thrown outside like a leper who has come to beg for scraps from the master's table. I crouch huddled in a corner outside the garage. With a dull buzzing in my left ear, I crane my neck and look towards the top of the driveway, to see whether his dinosaur Cressida, draped with the provincial health ambulance department logo, has left.

I spot him walking up the unpaved, unkempt driveway. As he reaches the driver's door, he sees me and wags his middle finger, firmly entrenching his dominance. In that moment I know I will never be brave enough to flee this house again.

He pulls away. I sit outside for what feels like hours. No one comes to look for me.

I wait until I imagine she must be in a deep sleep after nightshift. Then I make my way towards the back of the house and tiptoe up the steps to the back door. What if she wakes up? I stand against the back wall for what seems like an eternity. I cannot risk another beating. Finally, in careful, tiny movements I slowly turn the door handle and tiptoe inside. The small kitchen is empty. I glance towards the dining room and see her throne deserted; surely she is asleep. I creep towards the closed passage door and peep into the lounge. Her beloved children sit opposite each other in front of the television. They briefly peel their eyes away from the screen, look at me and without uttering a word return to their favourite Saturday-morning programme. I desperately need to use the bathroom. I close the door as quiet as a mouse, lean against the maroon tub in an effort to find relief from the pain that pulsates through every cell of my eleven-year-old body. I have an urgency that is beyond any wound, the reminders of the beatings I have endured. Leaning against the abnormally large sink, I slowly peel the atrocious mustard-coloured tracksuit pants off my bruised thighs and legs. Next comes my underwear. I can hardly contain myself from the odour that greets me. My pants are covered in faeces. I almost pass out from the stench. Shame drowns me. Still holding on with my left hand, I use my right hand to close the sink with the stopper and open the hot-water tap. I cannot risk disposing of my waste in the toilet lest I wake her. I need to wash everything in the same water and make sure that my mess dissolves enough to pass through the drainage system, leaving no trace of my shame.

I catch a glimpse of myself in the cabinet mirror. I look closely; there is no evidence of bruising or attack on my face. I stare into my sunken eyes. I am a stranger. I feel a cry rise in the walls of my throat, but it remains silent. I cannot make a sound. I drop my underwear in the water and begin to undo the mess.

My bruised hands ache as I scrub, but they are not as painful as the stench of my shame. As I rub the soap against the fabric, I am overwhelmed with a wish to disappear. How can my life have become this?

A few months ago I was living happily with Ma in a home where I felt loved. Hot tears of anger run down my face. I watch the muddy waters dissolve the remnants of my shame as it disappears down the drain. At the age of eleven I am ready and aching to die.

FIVE

Aftershock

The morning unfolds in a daze. The muffled buzzing in my head continues. I am terrified I have burst an eardrum.

No one speaks to me. I begin to tackle the heap of chores that awaits me. My mind finds escape in the lush gardens of my home in Umtata, my moral compass, my place of centred peace.

I lift my younger brother's daily urine-soaked gift to me and pour washing powder over it. I open the tap and watch how the water submerges his soiled towel nappy. He is a year younger than me yet The Mother still encourages him to wear these things and wet his bed, so that I can clean up after him. So that I will always know my lowly place.

As I scrub, I look at my swollen hands beneath the soapy water. Strangely, for the first time since my beating, the pain has lessened beneath the water. It's almost soothing.

I go outside to the back and hang the washing on the line. Slowly, I walk back up the few steps into the house, into the dining room, pull out a chair and sit down. My two younger siblings are watching TV as usual, spoons clattering merrily against their porridge bowls. I glance across to Tando sitting on the floor with his bowl in hand. There is no warm porridge for me.

My stomach makes a low growl. I close my eyes and imagine lifting a glistening, heaped spoonful of tasty wheat to my mouth.

The family walk past me to place their dishes in the sink. None of them notice me. I am a hungry ghost.

A few hours later, while I am repacking my clothes onto the two shelves allotted to me in the passage cupboards, The Mother calls out to me. I jolt in panic.

"Tilili?" I respond.

"Come here," she shouts.

Hesitantly, I open her bedroom door. I look down, terrified to lock eyes with her fury.

"I have called Umtata and told them of what you tried to do. They do not want you back and will be sending Nomhi [my Ma] to come tell you that. When Victor returns from work make sure you go to him and apologise for allowing the devil to manipulate you into thinking you could run away."

She is smug as she speaks, and my head stays hung in shame. My heart breaks to hear that my family does not want me. I briefly glance up to meet her eyes and sense her victory, her belief in the power she now has over me. She basks in silence, perhaps waiting for a response. I'm left to wonder whether to move or stay wedged between the wall and the door. I stay. I cannot move … I do not know how to leave or how to stay.

Finally she speaks: "Get out of my sight … and if you tell anyone outside this house about what happened here I will kill you."

I lift my feet and slink out of her bedroom. I finish packing the cupboards as quickly as I can, aware that any delays on my part might warrant a second Armageddon.

The Father comes home later that afternoon. Once again I am sitting outside on an old pot, next to the garage. As his car draws closer, I feel like a miniature David overshadowed by the approaching Goliath. I hazard a leap of faith and fix my eyes on his, hoping to catch a semblance of humanity. He lifts his right arm to motion that I should open the garage door. I gratefully oblige, leaping to my feet. I am relieved at any contact, any acknowledgement from the man who has beaten the shit out of me. I move aside and watch him inch past me; I long for a second sign of affirmation. As he parks, he stares ahead, as though I am invisible, his eyes focused on manoeuvring his silver car into the garage. When he walks past me into the house as though I don't exist, I realise I have been too eager to be forgiven. I imagine he will walk into the lounge, recline on his La-Z-Boy and call for Tando to untie his shoelaces as he always does. Then he will fall into a deep sleep, ruffled only by intermittent waves of cackled snoring.

I stay sitting on my pot outside for an hour, maybe two. No one comes to look for me. The last time I have eaten has been the night before. I watch the residents of kwaMagxaki scurry around, up and down the hill, getting on with the business of their day. I pick up a broken twig and scrawl the word *die* in the sand at my feet. I wonder why Tando, who was once my keeper, has not bothered to find me now when I need him the most. More hours slip by. I am now convinced that no one is going to ever come and look for me. What if they leave me outside forever? What if I am never offered a plate of food again? What if I die here? Will anyone look for me? There is no one who cares. The only one who may shed a tear will be Ma, but even she has forgotten me.

Finally, I summon the little courage I have left and make my way, once again, to the back of the house, up the few steps and into the kitchen. It is empty. I tiptoe to the dining room, briefly lifting my head to glance to my left, towards the lounge. The Father is awake, reading the newspaper. Eager to get the possible rejection out of the way, I quickly approach him.

"Bhut Victor?" My voice is barely a whisper.

He lifts his eyes from the paper and glances at me over the brim of his old-fashioned glasses with the square rims.

"I am sorry for what I did today. I promise I will never do it again."

He looks at me for a long time, his eyes drilling terror into my eleven-year-old self. It feels like an hour – in reality it's probably only thirty seconds.

In a last-ditch effort to show this man that I am truly remorseful as I have been commanded to be, I manage to maintain eye contact.

"Okay ... If you ever try that again, I will beat you until you wet yourself."

If only he knew.

I gather what little dignity I still have and slink out the front door that I'd been ring fenced into just this morning. I return to the pot outside, beyond the garage. My heart finally releases my gated tears. My pain is no longer physical. It is as if rejection and displacement have eaten away at every last bit of hope in me so that there is nothing left. I am a prisoner here, with these people who have beaten me into submission and fear, and all that I am left with is a big hole of shame and self-hatred within.

Finally, long after my last tears have fallen, I hear footsteps approaching and see Tando making his way toward me. He looks at me with such pity, his inability to rescue me clear in his awkward silence. He stands beside me without uttering a word, then walks back to where he has come from. Moments later he reappears, eyes darting behind him to check whether anyone's watching, then hands me a crumpled slice of brown bread. He whispers stern instructions: "Khawuleza utye esisonka ungekabonwa. Angakuboni uKaz ngoba angayosixela kulamama." (Eat this slice of bread quickly before anyone sees you. Make sure that Kaz doesn't see you as he will probably go and tell his mother.)

I gobble the bread in two ravenous gulps. I have almost forgotten just how hungry I am, since eating my last meal the night before. By the time I swallow the last chunk of his saving grace, my brother disappears back into the house, before he can hear my mumbled thank you.

Twilight announces its looming presence and yet again I make my way around the back, up the steps and in through the back door. Lungelwa has begun preparing the evening meal. In a whisper, I offer to assist her in peeling the potatoes. Perhaps if I make myself useful then the fury that still lurks might be forgotten. Perhaps The Parents will realise that I am not satanic after all and may welcome me back into the fold. I have never strung more than two words together to Lungelwa, let alone a sentence, yet now I find myself drawn towards her. I notice how swiftly she moves between the stove and kitchen sink; her usual shy demeanour vanishes as she takes control. She talks me through the tasks she delegates to me and heaps me with praise at the pace at which I comply. Occasionally she breaks into song, the latest Splash hit or a Dalom Kids number, artists I have never heard of before, but each note is like balm to me. In the kitchen I find myself drawn to her. She will no longer be The Help, but Lungelwa, my new and only friend.

As the day folds into darkness, The Mother leaves for nightshift and The Father and children retire to bed. The dishes done, Lungelwa, Tando and I retreat to the confines of our shared cave. Lungelwa has the bottom bunk; I have the top, and Tando the adjacent three-quarter bed. When I am sure Tando is asleep, I creep down the ladder and gently pat Lungelwa awake. Half asleep, she moves against the wall, allowing me space to creep in beside her. I gaze into her deep brown eyes. For the first time since I moved here, I feel a hint of safety. I snuggle into her bare chest. Her closeness and warmth evokes a deep tingling sensation within me that engulfs me from the crest of my head to the tips of my toes. I sleep.

I awake early to find myself alone in the bed I have shared with my newfound friend. I am immediately filled with pangs of shame at having allowed myself to feel this tingling for a woman, the same feelings I had for my cousin Minky all those years ago. I think of her breasts, the perfectly cupped scones on her chest. Why do they make my heart race so? I try to brush aside the thoughts of shame-filled desire and get on with the business of the day. I join Lungelwa in the kitchen without saying a word. The Mother soon announces her return from work. She bullishly instructs Lungelwa to teach me how to make the morning porridge as this will be my responsibility from here on out. I focus all my energy on each instruction, taking care not to show any signs of the attraction I have felt the night before, lest Lungelwa tell The Mother, who will this time in all probability bulldoze me to death.

○

Later in the day, a little before nightfall, there is a soft knock on the door. The Father opens it and in walks Ma. I am in the kitchen, deep in the suds of washing dishes. My heart races in leaps and bounds at the sound of her voice. I quickly retrieve my hands from the water, wipe them dry on my pants, but as I dash to greet Ma I feel The Mother's daggers of fury-spitting fire. Like a dog who's been whipped, I return to the dishes, taking extra care to ensure they gleam from my efforts. Ma sits in the lounge and engages in casual conversation with The Father. Finally, the dishes done, I sit in the kitchen, waiting for permission to move to the lounge.

I wait and wait and wait ... for nothing. I know that both Ma and I can do nothing until the Queen Mother, who rules with an iron fist like Stalin, announces her bedtime. Only after she removes herself from the company of her sister, who has travelled over four hundred kilometres to get here, am I finally granted a shot at bravery. I stand up and make my way to the lounge – only to be met by the sunken face and perhaps buried heart of my former mother.

"Hello, Ma ... How are you doing?"

"Molo, Star Locks. I am okay. Please take my bags to the bedroom."

She still refers to me by the pet name she gave me, Star Locks, but there are no hugs, no touching. A simple instruction, that's it. Hollow words. Silently I pick up her belongings and lug them to the empty bedroom and prepare to retire to my own. I am changing into my nightdress when Ma enters with my still slightly soiled but now dry underwear in hand.

"Why have you not washed your underwear properly?"

She has come all the way to ask me about my bloody underwear.

"Because my hands were too swollen and sore to rub it rigorously."

She leaves the bedroom without a word. Numbly I continue to get ready for bed. A moment later she returns and asks me to sit next to her on my brother's bed. She speaks softly but firmly. I see the pain in her eyes.

"I will not be staying for long. I came to check if you were okay. Things have changed and I will not be able to take you home with me. You belong here now and you need to try to blend in. Don't try to run away again. There is nothing I can do for you."

With that, Ma places her hand gently on my thigh, rubs it back and forth and then quickly stands to leave. As she opens the bedroom door, she glances at me once more and walks out. I stare at the floor; I am hollowed and numbed by the sorrow of her words. I have truly been forsaken.

This is the last time I will see Ma for a very long time.

○

When I wake the next morning I look out the large bedroom window to see Tando walking Ma up the steep incline, bag in hand. I have no more tears left to cry. My last hope is vanishing with the break of dawn.

I push the lace curtain aside, placing my hands on the glass in an already failed attempt to reach out to her. I watch again as she grows smaller and smaller, finally disappearing into the same horizon that whisked her from me before.

I descend into a black hole. I do not know if I can survive this house, this family. But somehow I manage to find a silent prayer: *If this, God, is a test of my sanity, let it pass, and as it passes, I too will have passed.*

I rummage through my school bag, find my A4 notepad, remove the back cardboard and begin writing down the days of the year from 1 to 365. At the end of each day I will scratch out the day that has passed. Each number that is ticked off will mean one step closer to a day of freedom. Somehow it makes sense to resign myself to a plan I can control on this cardboard. I count the years I will have to remain a slave. There are seven before my redemption: 7 x 365 = 2555 days. Today is nearly at an end. By the end of tomorrow there will be 2554. By the end of the week, 2548. And so I will myself on. Eventually the day will come when I will be free.

○

My twelfth birthday comes and goes unnoticed: no cake, no presents, no song. Throughout the day I hum the 'Happy Birthday' tune to myself. I am like a ghost in this house.

Without consent or notification, my surname has been changed from Danana to Mabenge and my Methodist faith replaced by the forced ritual of the Seventh Day Adventists. My once carefree self has been beaten out of me. I have been transfigured into an aged, lonely person dictated to by fear, unable to express my feelings, let alone my growing conflict with my gender. I face each day in subdued obedience, without curiosity or rebellion.

School becomes my only escape from the prison of home. I have developed a few friendships with some of my classmates and seek motherly affection from the teachers. I become particularly attached to Miss Stokes, my grade teacher. She is a jovial woman with curly auburn hair and makes my transition into the new school easy for me, making sure that I am up to speed with the work each day. She has placed me next to Vee, the only other black girl in the class. We spend all our time together and, as the year progresses, form a strong friendship with another classmate, Dianne. Our friendship allows me a taste of childish freedom away from my world of fear and domestic chores at home.

By the time the year draws to a close, I have become the resident shotput star, breaking the existing record, under the guidance of my science teacher and athletics coach, Mr Nel. I have never really participated in sport before but because sport is obligatory there is no alternative. That I do it well is a surprise to me. But soon this too will become a weapon that will be used to further deny me my liberties.

Academically, I have been performing reasonably well. It's been a constant battle to get homework and studying done while having to work through the long list of duties that are expected of me before and after school. I am constantly fatigued and, whereas I once excelled, my results are now reduced to mediocre. I hear The Mother gloat as she calls Ma and my grandparents to tell them how the school was right to make me repeat my grade as my unimpressive performance now confirms the inadequacies of my previous school.

The arrival of 1994 and South Africa's great leap to 'freedom' sees me move on to the final grade at primary school. The country has concluded the CODESA negotiations and a democratic dispensation is on the horizon. But nothing has changed at home. In the evening, I mark off another day on the cardboard back of my A4 pad. My goal is to make it from one day to the next with as little trouble as possible.

A small light breaks through the dark days after I successfully audition as a first soprano for the senior choir. This allows me to connect with my passion for music. It is the one and only passion I share with The Mother. She has an angelic voice, which finds me lost in its waves whenever she opens her mouth to sing. I watch as her lower lip quivers, her eyes firmly shut, as though she is travelling to faraway worlds where she is released from her cruel and callous human form. But these moments are short lived. As her last chord fades, the angel transmogrifies to black.

SIX

"You are a girl, not a boy"

Red. I stare at the toilet paper. Oh my god. I am dying. I am back from school one afternoon when I discover the stain of blood on the white paper. All day I have felt a heaviness, a dull ache in my lower back and abdomen.

I can hardly bring myself to look. My heart all but stops, strangled in terror. Am I dying? Do I need to tell them? Go to the hospital? I am close to tears but I know I have no right to cry here, let alone cause a scene that will surely warrant another beating.

I sit on the toilet for a long time. I feel like Alice tumbling down the rabbit hole, with no strategy or plan for my escape. My mind is a mess as I try to make sense of the blood. I have not knocked myself or fallen. Then suddenly it all starts to make sense. Perhaps I am growing a thing between my legs like my brother Tando and my boy cousins, the boy thing I long to have. Perhaps this is not such a bad or unusual thing.

I wipe myself again. More blood.

I carefully roll out enough toilet paper to create a plaster and place it inside my underwear. Maybe this can stop the bleeding.

I hastily flush the toilet. I need to find Tando.

"I have to tell you something." He is sitting outside on the steps at the back of the kitchen.

My words tumble out in whispered urgency. "There is something happening to me … I have blood coming out from inside of me."

A mixture of terror and excitement plasters my face. Perhaps Tando will confirm my evolution and assure me that this blood is now making its way out of me for a thing to grow between my legs.

"Oh no, you're having your periods. Yho!"

Periods? I have no idea what this word means, but it appears Tando does.

"This means you're going to have to get girls' sanitary wear and use them. You are going to have to tell lomama ngokwakho. I am a boy, so there is nothing I can do to help you."

First Ma, now him. This is the second time someone I have pillared my life on has told me there is "nothing they can do for me"; twice within the space of a single year.

We sit for a long time in silence, Tando and I. Finally I carefully lift my behind off the back stoep, check whether I have left a trail of blood, and walk cautiously back inside. I throw myself into the evening chores, cooking, washing dishes, all the time aware of the wad of toilet paper between my legs. Finally it's time to go to bed. Toilet paper in place, I try to sleep, hoping the new day will bring a physical healing, one that will not require a conversation with The Mother who will in all probability kill me for being a bleeding boy.

○

Two days later and the uncomfortable reddened plaster between my legs still makes for better company than the anguish I imagine trying to explain to The Mother what is happening to me. I panic when she makes a random remark at how quickly the monthly supply of toilet paper is running out. I try to muster some courage to approach her, but she's always either in the dining area, in her bedroom with her beloved kids, or asleep. Day three arrives. I commit myself to speak to her. The blood is increasing and the toilet paper is depleting at a rapid rate.

Truly terrified, I have begun finding creative toilet paper alternatives, using an old scarf, a T-shirt – I even cut up a favourite old jersey. I discard the soiled evidence of my confusion and shame in the outside bin, waiting for dark, making sure that no one sees me.

Finally I find a moment when The Mother is sitting in her bedroom, alone. Her children are preoccupied with stuffing their faces and The Father has returned to work. I have been mustering the courage in the kitchen, sitting on a chair with my legs closed tightly shut in an attempt to restrict the outpouring. I stand up, walk down the darkened passage towards her bedroom. I knock timidly. She summons me in. I look down as the floor.

"There is something I need to tell you."

Without lifting her head from her obsession, the latest Wilbur Smith, she asks what I need.

"Tando told me that I am on my periods when I told him that there is blood coming out from inside me."

I somehow manage to get words out.

"Oh! So you're the one who has been wasting our toilet paper."

My head, as if mechanically set to obey her tone, hangs in shame. I clasp my sweaty hands behind my back and take a step backwards to allow my back to touch the wall, my temporary shield for the beating that is sure to follow.

"Sies! You will bring me problems."

I stand in silence, waiting for her to help me resolve the problem I have been battling for days. Nothing. The minutes tick by, still nothing. Finally, deflated, I steal out of her room, back to the kitchen.

That night proves to be the toughest yet. I hardly sleep, tossing and turning into dawn, clenching my legs tight, careful not to over use the toilet. By the time I get to school I can no longer mask my discomfort from my teachers, let alone myself. I have become grumpier than usual and elect to sit alone. Every hour or so I ask to leave the class to go to the toilet where I change the blood-soaked toilet paper and place a new wad between my legs. When the bell rings for the mid-morning break my teacher asks me to remain behind. A wave of embarrassed despair and panic sweep over me at the possibility of her knowing the secret that looms between my legs. When the rest of the class has filed out, I head over to her desk, beads of sweat forming on my forehead.

"What is going on with you, my dear? Is there anything you want to tell me?"

I hang my head in shame and a massive wave of emotions threatens to betray my stoic demeanour. I shake my head from side to side.

"What is going on? Talk to me ..."

The second gentle plea makes it easier for me to lower my inhibitions. I shuffle my feet from side to side and I finally utter the words: "I have started bleeding between my legs."

She lets out of sigh of relief, followed by a chuckle that immediately places me at ease.

"There is nothing wrong with you! In fact, you're a very healthy young girl!"

She takes me to the nurse's office down the hall and relays my earlier revelation to the woman on duty and then leaves.

"I hear you've started your mensies. I will show you how to use a sanitary pad, as well as take you through the process of remaining hygienic at all times."

The nurse pulls a gigantic plaster from a packet and shows me how to use it, explaining how many times it must be changed and what my cleanliness routine ought to be at this time of the month. My eyes grow bigger with every instruction, as I realise that this bleeding will be something that will occur every four weeks for the rest of my life. Surely this must be a curse.

"So does this mean that I will not become a boy?" I can hardly hold back my tears.

She lets out a hearty laugh. "No, you are not going to be a boy. You are a girl. Your body is developing now and when you are old enough you will be able to carry children."

I feel a part of me wither under the burden of her words. My confusion grows. It seems that everyone is in agreement that I should be a girl. This has been the narrative since I was a child in my grandparents' home; this had been drummed into me by Ma, who is now my aunt, by The Mother and now the people at school. No one knows about the restless feelings that grow daily deep within me.

I walk out of the nurse's room and make my way to the bathroom. She has gifted me a pure white sanitary pad to replace my faithful sweater sleeve. The nurse's words linger in the back of my mind throughout the day: *No, you are not going to be a boy. You are a girl.* They will play over and over and over again for many years to come.

I arrive home that afternoon to find a few packets on my bed with the words "Dr Whites" across in a large font. I open one; they are not the same as the one the nurse gave me, but after reading the instructions I conclude these are indeed for me. I will bleed in silence and I will have to accept my fate. *You are not a boy. You are a girl. You are not a boy. You are a girl.*

○

The following year, 1995, I enrol at Pearson High School, having fulfilled the requirements for admittance to Grade 8. Tando is now in matric and it's decided that only one of us can have a school blazer, a mandatory part of the school uniform. It's clearly not me who's chosen, which gets me into trouble from the word go. The penalty for not wearing a blazer is detention after school. At home I am chastised and punished for "always being in trouble". Detention is a sign of "ill-discipline", despite all my detention slips clearly specifying the missing blazer as the reason.

My Von Trapp primary-school outfit is now replaced with a pale green skirt, white shirt and a black jersey brandishing the school logo with the motto *"Maxime Do Operam"* (I give of my best). How ironic, because without the compulsory blazer I am always at a disadvantage, no matter how hard I try to shine. To avoid detention, I am constantly trying to duck from the eyes of prying teachers as I walk into the school gates each morning. I am the kind of child who hates doing the wrong thing, so this induces a deep stress within me. Occasionally Tando lends me his blazer during school hours, allowing me moments of security in part ownership of a garment I am told I will inherit the following year, when he leaves school.

Despite my inner turmoil, I manage to present a 'happy child' façade during the school day, maintaining my close friendship with Dianne and Vee. But as I make new friends I am horrified to discover that I develop feelings of sexual desire towards some of my new female friends. The words "You are not a boy, you are a girl" haunt me. I try to dismiss my shameful feelings. I am consumed by thoughts of sin – the Church frowns heavily on sexual relations between females. To avoid going to church, I throw myself into sport, and most Saturdays are now taken up by athletic obligations. The Mother is on to me.

"Athletics is an excuse to avoid going to church. You must truly be the devil's child," she hisses her disapproval as I stand, tog bag in hand, athletics vest neatly tucked in beneath my inherited white tracksuit top. As she chastises me I hang my head in shame. If I show her how remorseful I am to be missing church again, then she might forgive me. Perhaps if I really excel on the athletics field, she will realise how great I am at shotput, at discus, and allow me an opportunity to compete with all my might. I regularly stand on the centre block of the podium, victorious in my age group. I am regularly selected for provincial trials. I wish that she could see me.

"Not only are you wasting your Saturdays away, but you are also taking Victor away from church. I don't know whether or not you realise that Victor is not your man, he is your father."

She will say this over and over again in the years that follow. The same way she will parrot her hatred for gay people. "If ever a child of mine turns out to be gay, I will kill them." Even if I could muster enough courage to tell her that I am attracted to girls, the threat of an early death prevents me ever from doing so.

I stand, heels digging into the ground, hoping to leave soon, but I cannot move until she is done with me. The Father emerges from their bedroom, hands me the keys and tells me to go wait in the car. A few moments later Victor emerges from the house. He is dressed in his usual beige tartan suit that has seen better days, the same white shirt, no longer as crisp, and his only pair of defeated side-slanting moccasins. We leave for the Westbourne Oval for my interschool athletics event.

We arrive in time to hear the announcer belch, "Girls' Under-16 shotput, make your way to the fields. Meisies onder ..." That's me!

"I'll pick you up here after church; hopefully your mother will have gotten over her petulance by then." With these words, Victor Who Is Not My Man drives off. It always amazes me how he can switch from confidant when she is not around to torturer when she is. As I run to take my place, I feel the ache of my too-small sneakers, the same pair I have owned since arriving from Umtata. It's all part of her plan to keep me in my place, to make sure I never believe I will amount to anything, reminding me that my fate is tied to owning no blazer and too-small shoes.

SEVEN

Going Home

To celebrate my grandfather's eightieth birthday, the whole Mabenge 'family' embarks on a journey to Mthatha. I have not been back in more than two years and my heart aches to see the house that was once my home and nestle within the walls of its safety. If only for a night or two. In the days leading up to the trip I am careful to keep my excitement well hidden lest The Mother changes her mind and cancels. As we leave PE in the late afternoon on a Friday after school, we make a detour past a dingy printing facility where she collects a few copies of a mini biography about the man who fathered her. It's titled *Amava onwele olungwevu* (The wisdom of grey hairs). As we finally set off, the sounds of ABBA hits brings a certain joy to The Mother as one track follows another, with 'One of Us' being a particular favourite. I sense we share a love for music and take this as a sign to learn and fall in love with her tastes in the hope that it will ease relations between us.

As we enter Ncambedlana, my heart quickens in anticipation. By the time we drive up the driveway and park on the lawn next to the vegetable gardens, it thumps in my chest. I am raring to escape the confines of the car to see Ma but retain my composure to conceal my excitement. As the engine switches off, The Mother turns to Tando and me to make an announcement. It's more like a warning.

"The two of you must not act like young children here. Don't you dare tell anyone about what goes on in my house or I will show you fire when we get back home."

It suddenly occurs to me that she is fully aware of the abuse to which she is subjecting us. We sit in silence waiting for The Father to unlock the car and release us.

We're greeted by a brigade of aunts I have almost forgotten, my grandparents and various cousins. Terrified that I may let something slip about my real life, lest she fulfil her promise when we return to PE, I move around emotionless, like a robot. Instead of embracing the people I have loved for most of my life, I opt to extend my hand for a firm shake. When night falls, The Mother, The Father and their two beloved children are allocated sleeping quarters in one of the outside flats at the back of the yard beyond the vegetable garden. My grandmother has tried to persuade the two young ones to join the rest of the youngsters in the main house, but to no avail. When they retire to bed a little later, I finally have a moment to spend with Ma. She calls me into her bedroom and asks after my health. I ache to tell her of the terrible abuse I am experiencing daily, but I remember Ma's words in PE after my failed escape: "There is nothing I can do for you."

But Ma knows me well and senses the reasons for my withdrawal and hesitancy.

"I know you are unhappy."

My tears brim on the edges of my eyes as I reassure her that everything is okay. I manage to say I miss staying with her and mention the onset of my mensies without revealing the horror of the details. On hearing that I have been given Dr Whites sanitary ware, she gasps in disbelief. And then there is a long silence. We both know there is nothing to be done.

When I retire to the children's bedroom, I finally fall into restless sleep, fully aware that in the morning I will have to return to my state of silence and submission.

The following day the birthday celebrations get under way. My Uncle JS is noticeably absent, which makes me sad. Aside from Ma, he is the only person I have looked forward to seeing. When I was younger, I used to pretend I was him when playing house-

house with my cousins. He was my role model, the man I wished to become like when I grew up.

When The Mother distributes the mini book she has compiled, she becomes the star of the show. She speaks eloquently about her father, while he sits across from her, beaming from ear to ear, lost in the memories of days gone by. Then we are instructed to perform a 'family item', a ritual associated with being 'members' of the Seventh Day Adventist Church. This pretence at piousness and love for our fellow man always leaves me feeling a measure of disgust in myself and the family I now belong to. If only people knew what lay behind the masks. I hate the fact that I have no option but to be part of the charade but I especially hate the dress code that I am forced to accept as "a girl", which consists mostly of below-the-knee skirts and all-concealing tops. I look beyond ridiculous, never mind the fact that I am always uncomfortable.

That night I go to bed filled with dread, knowing that we will be returning to PE in the morning.

I wake up early, at around 5:30am. During my restless night, I have devised a strategy that might delay our imminent departure, our return to the house of hell. I creep through the silent house to the kitchen to find my grandmother busy with her morning routine. I manage to distract her with uninspiring conversation while I steal a large breadknife from the drawer and hide it under my oversized sweater. I then make my way outside and wedge myself between The Father's car and the wall. With my heart pounding, I remove the knife from beneath my sweater and crouch near the rear wheel. I pause, scanning the surroundings for any imminent threat. Then I take a deep breath and plunge the knife deep into the tyre. I have not been prepared for the release of pressure, which makes a loud gushing sound. Within a few seconds the tyre is pancake flat. I breathe a huge sigh. Surely this will buy me a few extra hours at home, possibly even another night. Without looking back, I march back into the house, drop the knife in the kitchen sink and make my way back to bed and pretend to sleep. My heart is thundering in my chest.

We are scheduled to leave before the family makes its way to the regular 11am Methodist church service. As we lug our bags to the car, the puncture is discovered by The Father. But my dream to spend another night in the house of my beloveds is not to be. Within an hour the tyre has been replaced and we are neatly packed inside the car and on our way back to Lucifer's den. All I can think of as we drive the long and silent road back to PE is that, no matter how hard I try, I will never escape the trenches.

○

Back "home" the year creeps along much like it has the previous two years. Every night I continue to cross days off on my A4 cardboard. The routine is always the same; my efforts are never acknowledged and my brother and I continue to slave around the house, doing the best we can. Tando is nothing like the brother I knew in the early years in Mthatha. As youngsters, ours had been a relationship that had been nurtured under the guidance of our grandparents. One day he had been there and the next he had been whisked away by The Mother and The Father, much like how it had happened for me years later. When I arrived in PE I had been met by a sibling who was a ghost of the person I had known earlier. His eyes were now hollow and he hardly ever looks at me. We speak mostly in fearful, staccato tones as we decide on how to split the kitchen duties or who will do the washing or ironing.

There is one intimate moment when we connect on my second or third night in the house. In the same small room he hears my muffled cries deep into the night. The next thing I know he is gently shaking me and whispering a plea for me to hold on as things will surely get worse if she is to hear my weeping. At that moment I am oblivious of how true his words will turn out to be. But his gentle tone will carry me through many days and nights of hell that unfurl like a broken sail.

EIGHT

Purple Black Bruises

When school holidays come, there is no difference to the routine of chores expected from my brother and me.

Just as we do every other day, we wake up early to make sure that when the family wakes they will be fed and the house will be clean. We are on the same level as Lungelwa, although unlike the pittance she is paid, we never see a cent for our efforts.

When The Parents and their children wake up they are served their morning porridge. We spend rare idle moments between duties in silence while the beloved children stay glued to the TV, The Father lazes away on his aged La-Z-Boy and The Mother is mostly embroiled in the pages of the latest Wilbur Smith. On the odd occasion when us three are allowed to join the others in the living area to watch TV, we are expected to sit on the floor rather than on her precious faded pink armchairs.

But mostly we are confined to the kitchen. It is tiny, with hardly enough space for the three of us. One morning when the maize-meal porridge is almost cooked and the weather outside is gloomy, I am able to banish the usual gloom of being marooned here and my spirit is in a joyous space. Washing the dishes, I have spent most of the morning fantasising about a freedom that is just shy of five years away. I often see the house in Mthatha in these day dreams, the smell of Miss K's Mona coffee and the strains of Handel's

Messiah thundering from the speakers of my grandfather's VW Passat. But I no longer dwell on a physical escape. My fear has taught me well.

Back in the kitchen Tando and Lungelwa are deep in discussion about a matter in which I have no interest. Their conversation has escalated to a point where they are in disagreement and my brother keeps probing her, unaware that he has driven her into a fury. I am jolted back to reality when she gets up from her seat and falls to the floor. I start to panic as I watch her convulse, her body contorting violently on the floor. The Father, the paramedic, rushes in and tries to hold her down, demanding an answer from my brother as to what it is that he has done. The Wilbur Smith-fixated mother remains glued to her chair, the nurse in her unperturbed by the unfolding emergency. When the convulsions subside, I am instructed to walk Lungelwa to the bedroom and assist her to lie down and rest.

As we pass The Mother, The Father grabs Tando by the neck and begins beating him with clenched fists. As he's thrown to the floor, The Mother turns a page and continues reading. I descend into a crazed panic, terrified that The Father will surely beat my brother to death. With each blow that rains down on him he pleads for mercy. Finally, The Mother looks up from her book and becomes a ringside spectator as she urges her husband on.

I cannot bear to look. Instead I focus on getting Lungelwa to her bed and making her comfortable. Then I creep back into the dining area, in time to see The Father's gigantic size-12 foot collide with my brother's face, crushing into his jaw. Tando is lying on the floor in a posture of surrender. I cower behind The Mother, intent on saving my own life by not interfering. I am all too aware that any resistance from me will have the pack turn on me.

The second stomping is more intense and then I hear what sounds like bone shatter. The Father continues to hammer his son until he gasps for breath. When satisfied that "the lesson" has been learned, he walks away, dismissing Tando to the bathroom to clean himself up. My brother lies motionless, then slowly crawls along the blood-stained tiles. I am frozen.

When he finally manages to lift his frame from the floor, his face is battered beyond recognition. He staggers past The Mother who is once again glued to her book. As he passes me, I sheepishly turn away and return to the kitchen and sit on a chair, back upright and eyes fixed on my sweaty palms while I silently pray to a God who does not exist and has abandoned my brother and me.

Tando stays in the bathroom for what seems like a lifetime. When he finally emerges The Mother banishes him outside where he remains for the better part of the day. I am left alone in the kitchen to prepare the afternoon meal. Once it's done, I am instructed not to dish out for my brother.

I obey. I can do nothing but comply. I fear for my life. Going without a meal is nothing new. Depending on her mood, The Mother often wields power with food, depriving us of it, despite the fact that we prepare it. When dishing up, she regularly enters the kitchen, barking, "Don't dish up for yourselves!" We dutifully obey, our stomachs growling as we listen to the clanking of spoons as the rest of the family devours the food heaped onto plates. Like ghosts we pick up dirty dishes and wash them before retiring to bed with growling intestines to lull us to sleep.

When evening falls I am instructed to find Tando and tell him to come inside. As I walk out of the back door my heart shatters into a million pieces. He is crouched against the wall, like a beaten dog, in the same corner to which I was once banished. As I get closer I see how swollen his face is. He looks like a boxer who's been knocked out in the ring. He seems to be breathing heavily, battling for air. I am ashamed that I have not done a single thing for him. I look away and tell him he is to come back inside. Slowly he drags himself up and limps back up the steps, into the house.

I continue my duties for the day and, as evening settles in, The Mother instructs him to wash the dishes and ensure that the kitchen is clean before making his way to bed. He dutifully obeys. When bedtime comes, we all retire to our respective holes.

When we awake in the morning, my brother's face has swollen to almost double its size. On seeing him in the kitchen, The Father instructs Tando to come closer so that he can "examine" the outcome of his "insolence". I am shocked beyond comprehension. Terror inhabits my bones. The Father then dismisses him, convinced that the swelling will soon subside.

Two days later and Tando's face is triple its size. The bruises have turned purple black.

Finally The Father summons one of his younger brothers, a medical doctor, to examine Tando. He emerges from the bedroom where my brother has been held in isolation, a look of horror etched on his face. He takes The Father aside and, in whispered panic, instructs him to take my brother to the hospital ... His jaw has been broken.

Watching in alarmed silence, I feel a tinge of hope that surely this man is in a position to inform the authorities of what is going on in this house. Perhaps this assault, inhuman as it was, is the sacrifice my brother has had to endure to secure our liberation.

Hours later, The Father drives Tando to the hospital where X-rays reveal that his jaw has indeed been fractured. They return home as the sun is setting. Tando clutches a mountain of pain medication, a bandage wrapped around his contorted face. Later that night, when the house is in darkness and the abusers sound asleep, my brother finally manages to whisper what transpired at the hospital. Before seeing the doctors, The Father instructed him to say that he had been injured playing rugby. The doctors could not align his jaw because too much time had lapsed between the injury and his hospital visit.

In the still of the night, as darkness cloaks my brother and me, it finally dawns on me: not only are The Parents pure evil, but there is no one in the world who can help us. While the bruises take months to fade, our terror grows.

NINE
Body Shame

When I proceed to Grade 9 in 1996 I am gifted my brother's blazer. Tando has left school, having completed his matric. I experience deep jubilation as I arrive at school fully kitted out; finally I can blend in among my fellow scholars. At last I will not be punished with detention for not wearing the full uniform. It does not bother me that the blazer is more faded than the rest, and that it's third hand, having been originally purchased by The Mother from the school's second-hand shop.

School is where I excel, where I escape the house from hell. I shine both in academics and on the athletics field, where I am regularly selected for USSASA (United School Sports Association of South Africa) championships over and above provincial achievements. I fall in love with the school subject History and am drawn to my teacher Wendy Rossouw, who is also my athletics coach. She has finesse about her, is athletically built and extremely well spoken, and I seek both her acceptance and approval, something that is impossible to get from The Mother.

It is in the classroom where I find my voice so it's not uncommon to find myself at loggerheads with most of my teachers, especially Miss Rossouw as I feel a release from the clutches that claw me into silence back home. She has a way of both controlling my behaviour while also singing my praises and encouraging me when coaching me one on one on the athletics field. I desperately want to open up to her, confide in her about The Parents, the tingling sensations that ripple through me when I am around girls ... but fear gets the better of me. Threats to never utter a word about what happens at home have been drilled into my head, especially after beatings and the deprivation of food.

My brother, Tando, has been accepted at Rhodes University to study for a Bachelor of Accounting Sciences. In the weeks before his departure he and I hold our regular whispered late-night meetings. By now Lungelwa has left her employment and we are full-time domestic workers. Tando is worried about leaving me at the mercy of these unpredictable and violent people who call themselves The Parents. He promises to complete his studies in the shortest time possible so that he can find employment and move me in with him. I try to reassure him that I will be okay, but it is a lie. I am terrified of being left alone in the house of my abusers. However, I manage to put on a strong front and promise to hang in there.

The year has been one of good fortune for The Parents and we move houses from kwaMagxaki to the more upmarket suburb of Newton Park, not too far from the Greenacres shopping centre in PE. Kaz, the adored youngest son, is ready for high school, but he is enrolled at a different one to me. One afternoon we are all once again whisked off to Birch's where Kaz is kitted out with brand-spanking-new attire, including a new blazer and rugby regalia, despite his apparent lack of passion and excellence on the field. I am in desperate need of a pair of sneakers for my athletics; my squashed toes ache and throb in shoes two sizes too small, but I keep getting told that there is no money.

I marvel at the opulence of the house in Newton Park. Unlike its small cramped predecessor, the new house is perched on the top of a hill overlooking the majestic Mercantile Hospital. I am enticed by the size of this place, with an outdoor entertainment area that boasts a bar of its own. I have never had my own room, but now I am given one that overlooks a gigantic, sparkling blue swimming pool. Am I dreaming? Perhaps this new house will change everything. Until this day, I have no idea how hard the universe must have conspired in my favour to afford me such a haven where I could find time to reflect in silence, even if it is for brief moments when everyone else has gone off to bed.

As I stare at my new surroundings, I forget for a moment about all the pain and torture that have come before. But, in reality, that sense of freedom is short lived. My duties soon resume. In all my excitement, I have neglected to realise that, since Tando has left, I will now have double the amount of work to do. The house is much bigger and my duties now include cooking, cleaning the entire place, preparing and packing lunches, ironing and doing all the gardening.

Exhausted at night, after completing my school homework and before I fall asleep, I mark off the day on my A4 cardboard. According to my calculations, I have just over 1000 days left under the parental sentence. I commit myself to my reality and continue going forward as best I can.

Most nights I fall asleep dreaming of Linda Zini, a friend at school to whom I have been growing more and more attracted. To call her beautiful would be an unfair understatement. She is exquisite. She moves with the grace of a gazelle. We have grown close. Whenever I have rare funds to spare, I gift her with single-track CDs and written friendship notes. I can gaze into her sparkling auburn eyes forever and lose myself in a worldly love that leads to an arousal in my heart and between my legs. I always make a point of holding her hand whenever I am in exclusive company with her. This affection marks the start of a long and torturous internal journey with the self. By now I have abandoned all hope of ever becoming a boy, and I have been reared in the Seventh Day Adventist Church to believe that relations between two women are impious and will most certainly reserve me a VIP suite in hell.

Linda and I try to maintain our friendship as best we can, even after we complete matric. When I learn of her death in 2003, four years after I matriculate, at the hands of a deranged and violent partner I battle to forgive myself for never having conveyed the love I truly felt for her. It takes me years to make peace with losing her.

Back at school in 1996, my body is a minefield of unwanted changes, causing me grave anxiety and depression. My once flat chest has begun to balloon; there is no escape from the fact that I am developing into the woman I have been reared to believe I am. The sports bras I have been wearing to flatten my chest can no longer hide the two swelling growths. I loathe my body, and try to avoid looking in the mirror at all costs. This is the only measure of control I can exert over this outward form that is so foreign to the core of who I am.

I begin forging letters to avoid the mandatory swimming sessions during Physical Education classes. I am deeply ashamed to change in front of the other girls or expose my body in the pool. When my instructor threatens to contact The Parents to find out why I always have some or other ailment during the summer season, I pray harder than I have ever prayed to avoid being exposed. Thankfully, the Physical Education curriculum is phased out a few months later, but still my loathing for my developing body grows.

TEN

Sweet Sixteen

By the time I turn sixteen, it has been over four years since I left my beloved Mthatha. Most of my birthdays have gone uncelebrated except for a Shoprite cake to signify 23 April, the day on which I was supposedly born. But, in truth, that date has changed so many times that until today I'm still unsure what my real birthdate is. Nevertheless, I am told that my sixteenth birthday is a cause to celebrate.

Since she has registered for a specialisation in psychiatry with the Queenstown Psychiatric Hospital, The Mother has become a regular commuter between PE and Queenstown. In her absence, The Father is in charge. I am responsible for all the chores, with occasional domestic help from time to time. The Mother is usually away on weekdays, returning on weekends to immediately delve into everything I have done wrong at home according to her precious children who are always eager to expound her with exaggerated reports of how I supposedly ill-treated them during the week. Their accusations usually range from how I have stopped them from messing up the beds after I have made them in the mornings, to making them wash their own dishes after placing them in a clean sink. God forbid that I ask them to assist with household chores. At times I am accused of not wanting to talk to them or insisting on sitting in the front seat as we are ferried to school in the mornings.

Whatever they choose to include in their police reports will determine my weekend punishments. Beatings are a given – The Mother's favourite weapon is a glass bottle of Steri Milk.

A few days before my sixteenth birthday, The Father picks us up from school. Throughout the day I have been feeling seriously dizzy and nauseous. But it's more than just the conventional symptoms of illness – it's more like some strange sense of foreboding. I choose not to tell him. I'm scared of his unpredictable temper.

At home I immediately begin preparations for the evening meal, as well as the next day's Sabbath. I tidy the house and scrub the toilets, straightening the house for The Mother's return from Queenstown. After supper I spend some time in my younger sister's room, a ritual I have mastered on most Fridays in an attempt to gauge what possible complaints she might have tallied up against me. I have found this to be a useful tactic as I can try to smoothe things out by sucking up to her before The Mother arrives. We play a game or two of Solitaire before my headache and nausea force me to dash into the toilet across from her bedroom and hurl up my dinner. Something is terribly wrong. I heave, gasping for breath as I hold onto the toilet seat. When I leave the bathroom I hear my father's phone ring. I pick up panic in his voice. As soon as the call is over he summons us into his bedroom.

"Your mother has been involved in a terrible car accident just outside Grahamstown. I need to leave immediately."

The Father hastily departs with my brother Kaz on the 120-kilometre journey while I am instructed to take care of a weeping Ney. Almost immediately the sickness I've been experiencing all day miraculously lifts.

Hours later, towards the break of dawn, they return visibly upset. The Father informs us of the severity of the accident: The Mother is in a critical condition in Livingstone Hospital. He instructs me to alert my grandparents, who arrive from Mthatha a few hours later.

We are all then ferried to the hospital by The Father. Lying before us is The Mother. She is barely recognisable. She had been tossed from the car and has sustained a mountain of injuries beneath the white hospital gown that covers her battered body. Her clavicle is fractured, the left side of her body taking the brunt of the collision, and she has a gaping wound on the back of her head. My grandparents, both with tears glistening in their eyes, move towards their firstborn daughter and gently stroke her hand. My grandfather gazes into her eyes, asking her if she is okay. She opens her mouth in an attempt to speak, but her tongue has been injured so all she manages to utter are indecipherable grunts that sound like gibberish from a scratched LP record. For a moment I wish her dead, that the injuries are severe enough to take her out of my life, but I am immediately wracked with guilt. This feeling that I've carried all day now makes strange sense to me. It is as though my gut knew it was going to happen. What if I thought it up and caused it?

A few days later she is discharged from the hospital. My sixteenth birthday has come and gone. I do not feel in any way excited at the idea of The Mother coming home, hoping that she will spend much more time in hospital. Of course I have to make sure that the house is in pristine condition for her arrival.

The Father informs us that she will have limited mobility and it will take time for her speech to improve. He instructs Kaz and me to be 100 per cent hands on in assisting her with her many needs, including bathing her and walking her to and from the lavatory. But once she is home, something happens inside me … It's like I sense a shift in power. When she feebly calls out for assistance from her bed, I pretend not to have heard or I walk outside, pretending I am busy doing something else and out of earshot. The door of compassion in my soul is closed to The Mother. My bruised and beaten heart is cold to her.

Fear has killed any love there could have been. I know it's just a matter of time before she rises from her bed and resumes her path of cruelty.

Tando arrives from Grahamstown a few days later, accompanied by my older half-sister Nini – The Mother's daughter from a previous marriage – and her husband. My grandparents have already returned to Mthatha. It is a moment of joy I cannot quantify into words, seeing the brother I have missed so much.

I return from school the following day to find that The Father has ordered a special cake just for me. He informs me that it has all been The Mother's idea, who has insisted on a big celebration to mark my sixteen years on earth, deviating from the customary R20 cake in the past.

The feast includes piles of braaied meat, fizzy cool drinks and snacks. The Mother is still bedridden so we all gather in the bedroom to sing and cut the cake. I am elated. I experience joy for the first time in many years. I allow myself to forget that which has gone before and for a day I believe I am loved and cherished and that perhaps the accident has been the miracle I have been praying for.

It is not just me who hopes for change in The Mother. That evening, my half-sister Nini, Tando and I hold a brief meeting in my bedroom and in whispers unpack the fortune that seems to have befallen all of us at the hands of our mother's close brush with death. My sister marvels at how, after more than thirty years since she was abandoned, she has now been accepted by The Mother with whom she has always longed to have a relationship. Tando speaks of his relief at the amends he has made with The Mother and I voice my hope that I can complete my time in this house without further violence, cruelty and hatred.

But that night we are living in a dream world.

When she finally does regain her mobility three months later, she reverts to her old ways within days. Although she is not immediately able to resume the beatings, her tongue makes up for what she lacks in physical strength. It is as though the fury has been gathering while she has been bedridden and at the mercy of my assistance.

Like a serpent spitting, she takes to calling me a whore to my face, much like she has done to her siblings and own mother on the phone at times. As she spews her vitriol, I am convinced that she may be possessed by a demon. I remain silent, terrified that any response from me will unleash another beating.

The family she had been so eager to reel in when she was battered, bruised and bedridden is not spared her wrath. She is unable to work, so her fury is trapped in the house. Weeks turn into months and her permanent presence in the home takes its toll on me. I no longer find joy in sports or academics; my passion for music fades. Depression sets in.

As the year snails by I retreat further into my loner status, watching the clock, waiting for night, to cross off the day on my A4 cardboard.

ELEVEN

The Gold Suit

When 1 January 1999 finally arrives, the end is finally in sight. The countdown to my liberation has truly begun – I have only one year ahead of me before I matriculate and can move on to tertiary education at an institution of my choice. I wake up earlier than usual on New Year's Day and begin penning my last 365 days on the A4 cardboard. There is finally a sense of hope in the air.

Although I am deeply depressed at home, I have discovered my voice at school, especially in History class and pent-up anger from home finds a challenging playground in which I can vent. My small band of friends and I are branded the little 'Winnie Mandelas' for standing our ground, a fitting analogy given that we are in a history class and have been encouraged by Miss Rossouw to develop strategies to push back against the biased curriculum we are being taught.

Miss Rossouw initially presents a very entrenched view of how the history narrative she has been trained to teach should read. She believes in what apartheid truly stood for: the separate development of races. Over time, however, her thinking begins to broaden and she starts to encourage us to find strategies to tell our own tales – those that lie unspoken as the sacrificial lambs of a streamlined education system that opened the gateway for many black students to study at Model-C schools.

My rebellious spirit spills over into other classes, which results in me being a regular visitor to the principal's office. It becomes a common occurrence for the morning announcements to end with: "Will Yolanda Mabenge please make her way to the principal's office at the end of break?" I act tough, pretend to laugh as my classmates cheer me on, but deep inside I know that if The Parents ever get wind of this, I will be severely beaten, maybe even killed.

My frustrations explode in Miss O'Grady's Accounting class or manifest in blatant disregard of authority during Miss De Klerk's English lessons. I thrive on my bad-ass reputation because it affords me the attention I so badly yearn for. I become a ruthless wannabe thug who bulldozes her way through anything and anyone using whatever means necessary.

At home I find ways around the "Do not dish supper for yourself" nights. When the hunger pangs became unbearable I either steal a can of Koo beans to gobble behind the outside shed or, like the family dog, pick edible bits from the remnants left on plates. It doesn't escape me that the dog has a better life than I do, but I am determined not to be distracted and, despite my rebellious outbursts, I focus hard on my studies to see the year through.

I decide to challenge myself and enter the Provincial World Knowledge Olympiad. The Father has started trusting us to get home by ourselves, so we are given an allowance for taxi fare and sometimes a treat or two during school hours. I save most of these funds, which I then use to register for the Olympiad.

Six of us from my school have entered and so we find ourselves one afternoon in Mr Theron's Geography class. I race through the questions as fast as I can, fully aware that if I am not home by 3:30 latest, all hell will break loose. When the results come back a few weeks later I am surprised to have achieved the top ranking in the school and receive a certificate to prove it. (Over the next few years The Mother will destroy the commendation, among a host of other documents that mark my academic achievements.)

By the time mid-terms come about, I still have no idea what it is I want to study. When I mention that I am considering studying medicine, The Mother dismisses my desire as " not a viable option for me". A degree in English literature is also not good enough as it represents "dinosaurs" from my grandfather's era and will do nothing to enhance the reputation of the family.

When representatives from UCT arrive at the school, armed with application packages, I fill one out, leaving the 'Degree choice' section blank. I hope that if my marks are good enough I will be offered a place and by the time admissions come around I will have clarity on what I want to study.

When the rest of the matriculants begin faffing about the inevitable matric dance, I am deeply conflicted. I have no idea how to start the conversation with The Parents. But finally the pressures of outfits and dates force me to lower all inhibitions and approach The Mother. On a cloudy winter afternoon towards the end of June, she is sitting in her bedroom. I knock softly on the door and then walk in, not waiting for her permission to enter. She lifts her eyes from her Wilbur Smith, and glares at me above the rim of her glasses.

"Uhhm, I wanted to let you know that the school has informed us that our matric farewell dinner will be on 23 September, which is the last day of school for the third term."

Her distaste for me is clear.

"And what are you going to wear to this dinner and where will it be held?"

I gather courage and forge ahead.

"I was thinking of wearing a two-piece gold suit, pants and a top. I can show you what it looks like."

She offers me a cold stare.

I hasten my way back to my bedroom to retrieve the photo I have torn out of a magazine showing one of my favourite RnB artists, Brandy Norwood, dressed in a killer shimmering gold pant-suit number. I dash back down the passage and into her bedroom. She glances at the photos and gives a curt nod that I interpret as a sign of approval and advises me that she will give me the necessary funds. I have no clue how much it will cost or how much fabric will be needed. When I mention that the school has commissioned the services of a seamstress, whom most of my classmates are using, she informs me that Bulelwa from her church will be more than happy to make the outfit at no additional cost. I leave her room ecstatic, thanking her repeatedly.

On pay day in July, The Mother instructs me to meet her at a fabric shop close to Greenacres mall after school. My guard is down. I have begun to believe once again that maybe she has changed, that her maternal instincts are kicking in for this child blossoming before her eyes. We meet at the store and choose three metres of gold fabric. A few days later we take the gold fabric to the seamstress Bulelwa in kwaDwesi, measurements are taken and I am relieved to hear that the outfit will be ready for a fitting by the first week of September.

When August draws to a close I ask Sibz, a male friend, to be my date for the evening and The Father agrees to ferry us to and from the event in his giant Nissan Sani. The thought of asking a female friend has crossed my mind, but I remember the gay bashing a few nights prior when we were all sitting watching TV and the topic of homosexuality had crept into the conversation. The Mother had randomly announced that, "I will murder any child of mine who tells me they are gay." So I don't even entertain the notion of a female partner.

September arrives. My excitement is tinged with anxiety. I have heard nothing from Bulelwa and whenever I ask her during our encounters at church she assures me that everything is on track and that my outfit will be perfect by the time the big night arrives. A second and then a third week go by and still I hear nothing. When everyone else at school begins to boast about dates, shoes, accessories and dresses, I pretend all is on track with me. When I am asked to describe how I will look, what I will wear and how my hair will be done, I say, "It's a surprise," praying that no one can hear the panicked pounding in my chest.

A week before the dance, on a Sunday night, I decide to approach The Mother, who has again begun retreating into her cave. This unnerves me. She is so unpredictable. I find her sitting in her usual position on her bed engrossed in her Bible. Tentatively, I call her through the half-open door, begging for a moment of her time. She summons me in. I ask about the status of my outfit. She heaves a long-suffering sigh.

"I do not know what is going to happen. I no longer have money for you or your matric farewell. By the looks of things, you will not be able to attend."

I am floored. I choke back my words. My heart thuds and races.

I mumble a pathetic "Okay" and make my way down the passage to my room where I fight back tears and try to work out how a plan that had begun so well has been reduced to this. I wallow in pity for a few seconds before deciding to take the plunge and approach The Father in the hope that he might be able to salvage my situation, as he did a few years ago when my brother Tando was faced with the same situation for his matric farewell.

The Father is in front of the TV, face buried behind a newspaper, when I tentatively approach him. I am well aware that this is a risky move and could result in vitriolic revenge from The Mother.

"My matric farewell dance is coming up this Thursday and I have spoken to Tilili, who has told me she has no money for me to get what I need." I stammer the words out, trying to make sure that my tone is neutral because I know that this conversation will be quoted back to her verbatim. His eyes remain fixed on the newspaper. After a while he casts a lazy look my way, nonchalant.

"I do not understand why your mother has not said anything to me about this. She knows full well that I have funds that I can make available for this."

With hope surging in my chest, I quickly bring him up to speed about the outfit, the costs and the proposed logistics for the day. As the dance is on the last day of the school term, he agrees to pick me up at 11am so I can purchase all the necessaries in time for the big night. I convey my gratitude and make my way to bed, so relieved that everything has panned out so well.

The following evening The Father and Kaz accompany me to Bulelwa's house in kwaDwesi for a fitting before she adds her final touches. Kaz is like The Father's shadow and goes everywhere with him. We arrive at the house to find the seamstress in a jovial mood. She informs me that The Mother has called ahead to inform her that we are on our way to see her. While The Father and Kaz chat to Bulelwa's brother, she whisks me into her tiny kitchen and shows me the pants, which are near completion. My eyes beam with joy when I see the calibre of her work and, after a quick fitting, I am satisfied that they are a perfect fit. I enquire about the top and she tells me that she has taken it to a button shop to get the buttons covered with the same fabric. Though not fully satisfied with her response given how fine we are cutting this for time, she assures me that when I return the following evening the entire outfit will be ready for the final fitting and any minor alterations we may need to make.

We return the following night – only to find that nothing has changed. The outfit is still not complete and I am once again assured that it will be ready by Thursday morning. There are just two days to go before the big night. The same story is rehashed on Wednesday evening, but the naive and hopeful child in me laps up every promise that Bulelwa makes me, assuring me that she is on top of things and that I will look amazing the following evening.

When the big day finally arrives my spirits soar. I am ecstatic to have achieved such a tremendous milestone and am determined to enjoy the festivities that lie in store for me. When the school bell rings at 11am The Father is waiting at the school gate. He ferries a few friends and me to town and leaves me with sufficient funds to purchase everything I will need, including an appropriate hair-do. He drops us off in the busy city centre where we make our way through various stores looking to complete my mysterious outfit. Finally, we stop off at the hair salon.

I rely on my friends for hair and accessory advice and will emerge a few hours later with a breath-taking hairstyle. I see The Father pull into the parking lot directly in front of the salon, his side-kick Kaz firmly glued to his hip. They remain in the car as my hair gets its final touches. Finally, I open the back door and plonk my high-spirited self in the seat behind Kaz. The Father looks concerned.

"Bulelwa did not manage to drop your outfit off this afternoon. We'll need to rush to her place and you'll have to get dressed there."

My joy turns to angst, but I brush it off as just me being paranoid.

At her house we find her brother sitting in the lounge. A few seconds later she appears from the kitchen and hurries past us down the passageway. She mumbles an unwelcoming hello. A while later she returns to the lounge and apologises for some or other delay.

Eager to establish where I stand in all this confusion, I follow her to the kitchen. What I find there rocks my already fragile equilibrium. Lying on the table is a pile of uncut material. When I look closer, I realise that all that resembles the pants I fitted just a few nights earlier is the unpicked stitching on the edges of two pieces of cloth that are now placed on top of each other. They have been undone! I reach out to touch the fabric, hoping that this is a terrible prank and the actual garment will be somewhere beneath this pile. I find nothing.

I turn to her in disbelief, and ask her what has become of the outfit she assured me she had completed. My eyes implore her. How is this even possible? She looks at me for a second and mumbles that she can salvage the situation if we afford her an hour or two. I walk back to the lounge, my heart a well of grief. A few seconds later The Father stands up and walks into the kitchen. A moment later he is back, reassuring me that things will work out. My tear ducts burn, threatening to spill over. I try to trace the sequence of events back to June. How have things gone so wrong?

We wait and wait and wait. The clock strikes six, then seven, and eventually I ask The Father whether we can leave. I have been glued to a chair for more than two hours, broken only by the occasional pacing. I have done my time – I do not want this woman see me break down and cry. My mind tells me that this has been plotted from the start and the least I can do is to retain some pride and walk out her door with my held head high.

When we get into the car, I collapse in a heap of pent-up tears and bawl my soul out. The Father glances at me, uncomfortable at my outburst and begs me not to cry. He slowly backs his car out of the driveway as my cries grow louder; they have become like death wails. My body sinks deeper between the back seat and the leg room behind the passenger seat. I crouch into the tiny space, much like I did when I tried to hide from The Mother when she wanted to take me from my beloved Ma all those years ago, knees pulled up to my chest, eyes tight shut. My pain bays in agony; tears, held back so long, stream down my face. The sun has descended behind the late-afternoon sky. I am so stupid for having trusted her.

As The Father turns onto the freeway I feel his hand reach out to me and touch me. He holds it for a brief moment, gently brushing it up and down as if trying to remove an invisible blemish or soothe an aching injury. This is the first time he has ever touched me gently.

We continue in silence. My tears slowly dry up. When I am confident that I have emitted my last sob, I pull myself back up onto the seat and stare out the window, lost in the moving black tar that has no end. By now, The Father has worked himself up into a fury. He blames The Mother and her friend and mutters that he will ensure that she feels his wrath when we get home.

By the time we pull into the darkened driveway The Father has called most of his acquaintances, asking them to assist with a dress, an outfit, anything. He has some success with Colin, who has a friend who owns a boutique who will allow me to choose any of his dresses for the evening. I look at The Father who has shown more kindness in the drive back home than in the past seven years I have lived in his house. It suddenly occurs to me that The Mother's plan to sabotage my matric dance has more to do with the type of outfit I have wanted to wear – a suit rather than a dress – than the dance itself.

But I am resolute in my decision.

"I do not want to wear a dress. I have never wanted to. That is why I made my request clear right from the beginning. I do not want a dress ... The dance is over for me and I have accepted that."

By refusing The Father's offer, I have thrown caution to the wind and am willing to accept the consequences of my rebellion. I no longer care.

With that, I climb out of the car and feel a new surge of tears rise up in me. My anger is building up, and I can no longer hold it in. I propel myself towards my bedroom, deliberately defying The Mother who could end my life in a split second if she saw fit to do so. I throw myself onto my bed and bury my face in my pillow to muffle my sobbing.

When I look up a group has gathered in my room. The Mother's friend, our neighbour Tamlyn, is part of the contingent summoned to see me in my most vulnerable state. She tries to assure, explaining that her daughter has left for the same matric farewell dance less than 15 minutes ago. There is still enough time for me to make it there. I know that her kindness comes from a good place and is intended to calm me and rescue the situation. I am being urged to accept The Father's offer.

The Mother dashes out of my room and returns with her poorly assembled alternative: an off-cream blouse-and-skirt ensemble. She tries to convince me to iron it and wear it instead of my gold dream suit. There can be no greater insult. I look at her and drown out her voice with a conversation in my head. I muster what little courage I have left and convince myself to pull my act together. I then politely decline her offer and tell her that I feel Bulelwa has deliberately sabotaged my evening, and that I am happy to concede defeat.

I look her right in the eyes, steeling myself for the inevitable slap I expect to follow my blatant disrespect. But instead of retaliating, she spins around and stomps down the passage to her room, shutting the door behind her. I politely ask Tamlyn to leave and change out of the school uniform I have been wearing for the past 12 hours.

In the lounge I catch the start of *Generations*. I feel like such a loser for having believed so naively that any good could ever come from planning with a mother with whom I have no relationship. I blame myself for believing that she could ever want something good for me despite repeatedly reminding me that I will amount to nothing. I berate myself for being foolish enough to have thought that she ever had any intention of making me happy for a single night when she regularly sent me to bed hungry.

I realise then that this has been the plan all along, ever since The Mother insisted on contracting her friend, the seamstress. The Father keeps telling me how angry he is with his wife, so I decide to ask him whether I can at least attend the after party I would otherwise have been barred from. Being part of the Seventh Day Adventist Church, any type of partying is severely frowned up. He agrees almost instantly without checking with The Mother, and after a few interminable hours, The Father – accompanied by his ever-faithful shadow Kaz – ferries me to St George's Strand, where we are met by throngs of ecstatic matriculants who have converged at the beach lodge to dance the night away.

I arrive dressed in a pair of jeans, my matric sweater and black shoes. On seeing my friend Lethu, I break down as I retell her the events of the past few hours. She embraces me as The Father watches from behind the wheel of his car. Lethu approaches him and asks The Father to allow me to spend the night at her house. For the second time in my life, he agrees without hesitation and leaves with his side-kick.

The following morning The Father picks me up from Lethu's house. Having gone all out to drown my sorrows – oblivious to the fact that sorrows swim well – and ravaging my insides with raw Spiced Gold Rum, I have a blinding hangover. I claw my way into the back seat of the car, mumbling a near-incoherent greeting. Lethu chats a little to The Father, assuring him that we have had a great time and that I am okay.

The moment we pull into the driveway at 5 Sargent Crescent my heart, as though on a timer, lurches, drenched in sorrow. A single night of precious liberty has come to an end and I will now have to deal with Cruella all over again. We enter through the back door, and I am suddenly panicked; she will know that I have spent the night at a friend's place, and that is sure to elicit a tongue lashing or even a beating. Over the years I have learned to put nothing past this woman. I am pleasantly surprised, though, when she greets me with a smile and a warm hello. I freeze, instantly distrustful, not knowing how to respond or where to look. She asks me how the party was, and I tell her it was fun. This is the nicest she has been to me in the seven years I have been in her care.

But her warm disposition does not last long and soon she retreats, to mope behind her closed bedroom door. I resume my duties, making sure to cook and clean as expected, despite my hangover. When I dish up for her she refuses to eat.

The stand-off continues for five days. By Friday evening, I suspect she must have grown tired of the silence. As I am preparing to go to bed I sense her follow me down the passage to my bedroom. By the time I take out my pyjamas, she is standing in the open doorway, hand on the door handle.

She calls my name. Her tone is her usual boisterous and commanding one.

"The time for you to wallow over unfinished matric farewell outfits is over now. You need to stop feeling sorry for yourself and get over it."

She's back. That is The Mother I have come to know, the power monger who needs to remind me of my place. I instinctively drop my head in shame. She asks me if I understand her. I respond sheepishly with, "Yes, I do."

And with that, she marches back down the passage to the lounge and takes her seat in the armchair next to The Father, who has returned to zombie status. That moment confirms that there will never be any love between The Mother and I. Whenever I find myself battling to hold on, I will return to that night and remind myself that my sentence is almost over and I need to get over it.

TWELVE

Feast and Famine

Towards the end of my final year at school, the Road Accident Fund pays out a hefty sum to The Mother in response to her claim following the car accident she barely walked away from in 1997.

This wave of financial fortune creates a happy home façade. Despite the re-emergence of her Dr-Jekyll-and-Mr-Hyde persona, The Mother's progress back to health has been quite remarkable for someone who was on the brink of meeting her maker. Suddenly we are regulars at the King Edward Hotel in Central and Protea Hotel in Summerstrand where it is almost mandatory to stuff our faces on the endless buffets. The spreads include succulent beef cutlets, lamb, grilled chicken, a huge array of salads, breads and delicious desserts. I am the first to take advantage because I never know when I might be scrambling for scraps and leftovers.

Sometimes I wonder whether I don't gorge myself at the buffet table as a way to avenge the humiliation she caused me over the matric dance debacle. But life continues, and I have managed in my own way to survive being the laughing stock of the entire matric grade. Over the years I have learned to select my truths carefully, so when anyone asks me about the events of the night I lay the blame exclusively at the hands of an unprofessional seamstress, making sure that The Mother is never considered part of the sabotage committee. Me keeping the true nature of The Mother to myself is integral to keeping up the façade of her in public, of her as saint and rescuer. This is the sick narrative that has been hammered into my head from the outset.

Back at home, however, although I am allowed to accompany the family to church and lunches or dinners at hotels, The Mother is extremely skilled in making my second-class status very clear. She constantly reminds me how she has been my saviour, rescuing me from poverty and the vices of my grandparents and aunt. If not for her, I would surely have ended up a disease-infested whore with no future. An interesting narrative, considering that she is the same person who constantly reminds me that I will never amount to anything.

Tando arrives back home from Rhodes while I am writing my final exams and is eager to find out if I have been accepted at the University of Cape Town (UCT). At this point, I haven't bothered to submit an application to any other university. My heart is set on UCT. The Mother has insisted that I apply to the local Nelson Mandela University (formerly the University of Port Elizabeth), but I resist – I desperately need to get away from the deadly hold she has over me. If UCT does not pan out, I will try my luck at running away again and this time I'll make sure that I succeed.

On Tando's return he is in high spirits and has an air of liberation and worldliness about him. But the years away have drawn us apart and I soon discover that his outward confidence is hiding what is really happening in his life. I discover he has dropped out of Rhodes University and has returned home for an indefinite period. When I ask him if he's failed the year, he brushes the issue aside. This realisation makes me extremely sad. What happened to his promise of finishing his degree and coming back to "save me", the plans to get a place of our own? Now he is back in the dark fold of his abusers, seeking to make amends with the very people who, over the years, have repeatedly beaten him to a pulp and hammered his head with tales of his inevitable failure.

In truth, he has returned a shadow of his former self, with a heaviness in his step. The Mother is furious at his failure and refuses to talk to him and when The Father is not around I am instructed to deprive Tando of food. He is confined to an outside room the size of The Parents' en-suite bathroom and is mostly barred from entering the main house or using the swimming pool. Whenever we have to go somewhere as a 'family', he is always excluded and the house is locked so that he cannot access either food or the bathroom.

While Tando is holed up like an unwanted dog in the room outside, The Mother rages about how she has been right all along about his devilish ways and that he will truly never amount to anything. She continually boasts about her perfect son, Kaz, who has been earmarked as heir to The Father's legacy and has made her proud in all aspects of her life. Over time I learn to use all the negations she utters to empower myself; it occurs to me that the only way to prove her wrong is to ensure that I do not fall prey to the same trap that has swallowed my older brother. So I study really hard for my finals and make a covenant with God that if He truly does exist and does in fact care about me, then He will get me into UCT. I make an oath to live by my truth and the magic that can be found in my heart.

When the call comes I have been sitting in my room staring at my cardboard calendar reflecting on how amazing it will be to scratch out the last day when it does finally arrive. There are but a few weeks to go.

The Mother, brash as always, shouts at me to answer the phone and jerks me out of my reverie. The telephone is in her bedroom so that it cannot be subjected to misuse, so I gallop down the familiar passage towards her open door. She holds the receiver in her hand and, before handing it over, she tells me someone from the University of Cape Town who wants to speak to me.

"Hello?" My voice quivers.

"Hello, you are speaking to Heather from the UCT Admissions Office. We received your application forms and final matric results and would like to offer you a place at UCT. You need to decide now what faculty you want to register in as you have made no selections on your form."

My heart leaps in loops of joy. I struggle to speak with The

Mother towering over me, watching my every move with a hawkish glare.

"Thank you, Heather. I'm not sure which faculty I would qualify to get into." I take a long pause. "Actually … I think I'd like to do an LLB."

"That is an excellent choice. We look forward to welcoming you next year."

When the call is over, I cannot contain my excitement – I am beaming from ear to ear. In truth, I have never really given an LLB much thought save for the times The Mother has insisted that I study law. In this moment, as she glowers at me, it makes sense to abide by her instructions.

What transpires next further shatters my understanding of the woman I thought I had got to know, multiple personalities and all. Just when I thought I had figured her out and nothing about her could surprise me she ups the stakes. She begins calling everyone, from my grandparents and aunts to her in-laws to boast how well I have passed and that I have been accepted at UCT to study towards an LLB. I stand in the passageway listening to each of her animated conversations. Had I not lived with her mood swings and inexplicable cruelty, I would have believed that she was genuinely happy for me. Listening to her euphoria I realise that this woman is even crazier than I had thought. In a split second all her rants on how I will never amount to anything, that my future is doomed and that I will die an Aids-infested whore due to my upbringing shifted to what can be described as a parent's moment of pride.

Within no time a family holiday is planned to Cape Town to 'orientate' me into my future surroundings. The car is not big enough to fit everyone, so Tando is left behind and given a consolation R500 to survive on, while the rest of us will be living in the lap of luxury in Cape Town.

On the evening of our departure, we pile ourselves into the Nissan Sani and pull out of PE in time to catch the sun descending on the horizon. I keep myself occupied by fantasising about the following year, imagining what my new environment will be like. It is all I can do to distract myself on the long journey.

When we finally reach the Mother City it is well into the early hours of the morning. We have been booked into the Protea Hotel in Gardens near the CBD. The view from our seventeenth floor is majestic. I gaze across the city and the sea and harbour bathed in soft morning light, marvelling at the perfection of its backdrop, Table Mountain. We are allocated two rooms, one for the adults and the other for the children, and soon venture out to experience the beauty of the city that will become my escape and reprieve within the next few months. We embark on an expedition to the harbour and spend the next couple of days sightseeing and acting like a happy family. When the camera snaps, freezing the moments in time, the pictures present a perfect family of broad smiles, white teeth and raucous laughter.

○

Back home in PE, the finances and logistics of my registration at university soon become a thorn in my side. I have not thought beyond the application phase and although I am pleasantly surprised that there is no required registration fee, there is a mandatory thirty per cent payment of the annual tuition fee of about R15 000 to R20 000 due by the end of March 2000. My heart sinks when I receive this correspondence and immediately I begin to doubt whether my dream to pursue my studies will ever become a reality. I brave my fearful heart and hand the letter over to The Father who has always made it clear that no child of his will ever be denied the opportunity to study. Fortunately, The Parents are not privy to the fact that UCT is the only institution I have applied to. The Father assures me that all monies due to the university will be paid timeously. The morning after the letter arrives he sends a driver to pick up The Mother from work and together they come to fetch me to accompany them to the bank. It dawns on me that The Father has requested her to spare some of her accident fund fortune to sponsor my schooling.

The ride to the bank is interminable. Not only does The Mother make it clear that she is doing me a huge favour by investing so much of her money in a child who's been destined for failure, but also insists that when I arrive at UCT I am not to make friends. "It's always better to remain antisocial than to have friends and that is what you need to become – antisocial." That is her instruction to me. I am in no position to argue.

When the monies are paid over to UCT and I am certain my slot has been reserved, I start weaning myself from of the family unit, extricating myself from the façade and isolating myself more and more. The weeks become days as I count down my journey to freedom and, eventually, my final day in PE dawns – and with it a host of unexpected emotions.

I wake up early to pack what little I have into a black suit carrier I have inherited from The Father. I have been spared a few hundred rand to spend on a backpack and some casual clothes to wear to lectures. The items are few but at this moment I feel as though they will fill to overflowing the biggest closet ever made. When I am done packing, I resume my daily routine of cleaning, if only for old times' sake. I convince myself that I have made it thus far and should savour every moment until the last.

The Father has not been able to secure leave for the day, so our departure for Cape Town is scheduled for later that afternoon. The entire family – minus Tando, of course – will once again escort me to begin my adventure in the city of Cape Town. Before our departure, The Father's eldest sister arrives with a litany of advice on how I ought to carry myself around boys and, when the time comes for me to engage in sexual intercourse, to always insist on using condoms. I cringe; I want the earth to open up and swallow me. Such topics have never been discussed in this house. I offer no response and merely look at her, nodding my head, but I am upset. After she waxes on about how "We are very proud of you as the first Mabenge to be accepted to UCT" I switch off, watching her lips move and her hips sway from side to side until she's finished. After her monologue, she hands me a crumpled R20 note and bids me farewell.

As soon as The Father arrives, he instructs us to pack the car, and we pile ourselves into the Nissan parked in the narrow driveway in front of the garage. As usual, I sit directly behind The Father, with my sister Ney between my younger brother Kaz and me. Tando has helped loading our belongings and, although I am about to embark on my dream escape, I cannot help but feel a tinge of sadness at leaving him at the mercy of the same folk who just a few years earlier almost killed him. It is clear that the responsibility now lies on me to continue working hard so I can take over the dream we once shared of finding our own place or possibly returning to our beloved Mthatha.

We pull out of the driveway and, in silence, embark on the 780-kilometre journey. I am lost in thought, contemplating the unknown of what lies ahead, when I am suddenly jerked back to reality by a bark from The Father.

"Have you not heard your mother's question?"

"No, what was she—?'

Before I can finish, he brakes in fury and the car comes to a screeching halt. Screaming profanities, he wrenches open the compartment between the front seats and pulls out a metal gear-lock. In a single, swift motion he turns on me and bashes it down on my left knee nestled against his back rest. As he hammers his blows, I am frozen in horror. The pain is excruciating, but I know better than to cry out. I crumple into full remorse mode, a stance I have learned to perfect over the years. When he is done, he adjusts himself to face the front, starts the car and resumes the journey.

But within seconds his rant begins again, and turns to look at me directly, as the car swerves across the road. He calls me names that I have become accustomed to: "Uzibonakalisa ukungabi nasimilo. Zizimbo ozifunde kwabanomokhwe bakukhulisileyo" (You are showing signs of insolent behaviour. These are the traits of the whores who raised you.)

At this point, I am consumed by terror that he will turn the car around and head back to the house of horror in PE, crushing my dreams of escape to CT. But he is brought back to his senses as The Mother screams that he is about to veer into a massive tree on the side of the road. The car squeals to a harsh stop for a second time and he glares at me in the rear-view mirror. I do not know whether to look back at him or continue to keep my eyes down. He, however, resumes his rant.

"You are sitting here daydreaming when your mother asked you if you had drawn all the curtains in the house. Instead of responding to her your mind is already thinking about the lascivious behaviour you will engage in when you get to Cape Town. Next thing you will return to us with a bastard child or full-blown Aids."

The Parents' obsession with Aids and "whoring" never ceases to amaze me.

I keep my thoughts and emotions bottled up inside. All I know is that these two sick and twisted beings cannot possibly be my true parents. There has to have been some mistake.

We resume the journey in stagnant silence, me staring out the window as the kilometres are swallowed up and the night sky grows black. The stars that sparkle above remind me that the world is much bigger than the occupants of this car. And that soon, soon I will be free.

THIRTEEN

Cape Town

We arrive at the Protea Hotel in Durbanville in the early hours of Saturday morning. After a few hours' sleep The Mother wakes us and instructs us to prepare to go to a church in the township of Langa where I am to be introduced to the congregation and entrusted to them for the year that lies ahead. How ignorant are they to think that I have any intention of attending their church once I have broken free of their shackles.

Once back at the hotel, we once again spend the afternoon stuffing our faces with delicacies on the buffet. When evening comes, we retire to our respective spaces. A tumult of emotion consumes me. Just before I drift off to sleep, it occurs to me that I just might have made it. That there is only a single night between me and a world undiscovered. Soon I will be at liberty to walk unknown streets and talk to whomever I want. To think my own new thoughts.

The mood around the breakfast table the next morning is sombre. I stay withdrawn – it's safer that way because I need to remain in character until I've been dropped off at res. We pack up and check out and soon we are on our way to Liesbeeck Gardens in Mowbray, where I am to take up residence.

The place is a hive of activity, swarming with students. I feel a surge of both nerves and excitement. I have never had carte blanche to engage with so many different types of people. Once I have been assigned a room, embarrassingly accompanied by the entire family to drop off my belongings, I walk them out, eager to begin this new chapter of my life.

◯

Once the family has left, shit gets real. I instinctively retract into my shell, but I know that I desperately need to find a way to interact with all these strangers around me. I am accommodated in a four-bedroomed flat and allocated the biggest room because my flatmates are yet to arrive for check in. The Parents have begrudgingly left me with less than R100, with instructions that it will have to last me for the remainder of the month, inclusive of toiletries and anything else I might need. I have never lived on my own and have no idea whether the amount is sufficient or not. Instead of feeling free, I feel terrified. I spend the next two days holed up in my room, barely stepping out other than to use the toilet and fetch a glass of water from the kitchen. I have no idea where the dining hall is, let alone how I am supposed to get to Upper Campus for orientation or lectures. On the third day, hunger pangs get the better of me and I make my way to the reception area to ask for assistance. It's a long hard walk that demands enormous courage. I feel like a mouse stuck in a mammoth maze.

Slowly, as days trickle by, I muster up the courage to start awkward conversations with my flatmates and other first-year students who have been allocated to this second-tier residence. When lectures officially begin, I make my way to the student residence allocation unit to request a transfer to a first-year residence. But when they pull out my file and look over my credentials, they inform me I applied too late so I cannot be reallocated despite having done so well in my matric year: a pass with matriculation exemption and distinctions in Maths, History and Accounting.

The Father has given me his old Ericsson 'changing faces' cellphone and regularly makes contact during my first weeks in Cape Town.

He assigns his PA to check in with me most mornings to ensure that I have woken up and am on my way to class. His façade of concern confuses me. The Mother, on the other hand, makes no effort. Slowly, however, I begin to feel trickles of freedom. I have set a goal to complete my tertiary education in record time so that I will never again have to be in the company of The Family of Four. My over-eagerness, though, blinds me to the challenges that lie ahead.

As Easter holidays approach I am suddenly flooded with calls from The Mother. She makes it clear that it is mandatory for me to make my way to PE for the holidays. It feels like I have no choice. My chest tightens at the thought of returning 'home'. When I naively suggest to rather return during the longer winter break as I could use the shorter holidays to ensure that my work is up to date to begin preparations for the mid-year exams, I regret the suggestion the instant the words leave my mouth. She slams the phone down on me.

Almost immediately, she calls back. Her tone is cold.

"I am not asking your opinion – I am telling you that you will return during the Easter holidays. Remember, I can destroy your education – and your life – with a single phone call to the university."

I have no choice. I make my way 'home'.

○

Despite my dreams and good intentions, I barely make it through my first year. I cannot shake the constant anxiety, the dread of returning to PE to spend every break and holiday there. Going 'home' unravels the fragile gains I make at building my self-confidence. Nothing has changed there. Every time I go back, within hours of arriving, I am expected to pick up where I have left off – washing, cooking, cleaning ...

I am in deep conflict with my other self, the young independent person I am growing into in Cape Town. But I am also imprisoned by my reliance on the family for my finances. I have still made no effort to seek an alternative source of funding. It unnerves me to listen to other students talk about their sponsors and donors; I have no idea where to even start applying. When I do finally manage to muster up courage to visit the funding office, I soon realise that The Parents will have to be signatories on the application forms.

By the third semester I have found my groove with people, socialising and making friends, reawakening the boisterous persona from my high-school years. I become a regular at a pub called the Pig & Swizzle. I start drinking and missing classes. I am overwhelmed by my freedom and overjoyed that I am finally fitting in. So instead of keeping my head locked in books and spending my spare time in the library, I forget to hand in assignments; instead, I socialise and skip lectures.

I also spend a lot of time getting to know a girl called Thandi Klaas. I'm instinctively drawn to her when she greets me one icy morning as we sit on the boundary fence of Liesbeeck Gardens, waiting for the shuttle to ferry us to Tugwell where all our meals are served. She has a face like a sunbeam and a killer smile with a cute gap between her front teeth. Thandi is a social butterfly – she always has a crew of girls with her – so I feel special when she extends an invitation my way to sit with them during mealtimes. We share a lot of the same subjects and soon we begin attending lectures together. On weekends she usually has friends visiting from other universities and technikons who stay over. I, though, would much rather have her to myself, so as soon as people descend on her place I hide myself in my room or nestle in the oversized chairs in the residence common room, watching TV.

One Saturday evening, lonely and bored, I decide to take a walk to Thandi's flat, which is directly below mine. As is our custom, I knock on her window but, instead of her face, I am met by one of the most beautiful women I have ever seen, Tash. My hormones go into overdrive and within no time my heart is pulsating joyfully against my chest. Thandi's face appears through the window frame a few seconds later. I mumble something like, "I just wanted to check up on you ... Will see you later." I walk back up to my flat, slam the door behind me and nestle into a foetal position and cry myself to sleep, ashamed at my response to the beautiful stranger. I am in turmoil about the feelings this woman has evoked in me. The Mother's voice torments me. I keep telling myself that my feelings towards women are extremely immoral. The desire to be a boy has long been suppressed, and whenever it threatens to resurface I force myself to focus on the normative of who I ought to be and who I ought to be attracted to. My only consolation is that I no longer have to wear skirts or dresses. I am now free to roam around in shorts and jeans – until, of course, I go home for the holidays, when I need to dress as a girl.

FOURTEEN
Going "Home"

Back in PE my brother Tando is still living at home. He calls me on the odd occasion to find out how I am doing and what life in Cape Town is like. By the time he phones one afternoon towards the end of the third semester, I have abandoned many of my social anxieties and am partying up a storm.

"You coming home these holidays?'

The very idea fills me with dread.

"I'd really prefer not to. I don't see why I have to come home every single holiday."

Tando's response is unexpected.

"If I were you, I wouldn't return. Remember, Kaz is having his matric farewell during that time. The Mother has gone all out to make sure he has everything he needs. Everything. His outfit has already been finalised."

I swallow back the memory of my own matric dance debacle.

Tando ends our conversation with, "If you don't want to suffer another heartbreak, it's best you don't come back these holidays."

That's all I need to hear to make up my mind. I will not return home. I know, though, that I will have to deal with the consequences of openly defying The Parents. When The Mother calls a few days later with instructions to leave Cape Town as soon as lectures are over, I boldly advise her that I will not be able to return home as I have an assignment due on the first day of the final term and I will not be able to access the material I need from PE. Surprisingly she concedes. I sense victory.

As the year draws to a close, I spend most of my time hustling for my next beer or cider with the little food money I am sent. Each morning I wake up early with good intentions to brave a lecture or two, but I inevitably make my way down Jameson Steps, past the law faculty, through the grounds of the Baxter Theatre, to buy a pint at the Pig.

I cannot, however, avoid going home for the Christmas holidays. After my final exam is written, I make arrangements to store my belongings in the facilities the residence has provided us. I have a deep-seated fear that I might not be returning the following year. I am sent a bus ticket reference and soon I'm on my way back to Port Elizabeth.

The Father picks me up the following morning at the Translux bus station. He seems almost happy to see me. We arrive home to find The Mother seated on the front stoep gazing dreamily at the harbour on the distant horizon. I resume my submissive persona and approach with caution to greet her. She takes me by surprise as she marvels at how I have got slimmer and how healthy I look.

Although I am happy to see Tando, it concerns me how comfortable he has become with playing the second-class son. We manage to find a brief moment alone and I quickly tell him about my newfound obsession with alcohol, which I assure him is just an in-between pastime when I am not in class or the library. I cannot tell him the truth, how I've developed an obsessive crush on my crutch Miss Booze. Within hours of being back at home, I am aching to reunite with her.

Within a day of being back, I am drilled back into the home routine of chores and below-the-knee female attire that I have abandoned for pants and shorts at UCT.

Along with my new affair with booze, I have also become entranced by cigarettes and now back home the cravings are grating my tits. Out on an errand one day, I spare enough change to rummage through the dusty streets of Korsten and find a Somali vendor who sells my chosen brand, Gauloises cigarettes, which in all honesty taste truly horrible but make for a much cooler image than the Styvie Blue or Benson & Hedges everyone else smokes. With my lungs puffed to satisfaction, it dawns on me that I need to mask the acrid smell of smoke. My newfound Somali friend has assured me that his trusted lose menthol smoothies candy will do the trick. By the time I get home I am feeling all kinds of nauseous from the chain smoking and paranoid that the stench of cigarette smoke will betray me. No one notices and soon I am taking regular strolls around the back yard, finding a tiny lane behind the tool shed to satisfy my daily nicotine cravings.

Just after New Year my first-year results arrive by post. The letter is addressed directly to me. The Mother, who has noted the UCT stamp on the senders' envelope, summons me to her room. She instructs me to open the letter and inform her of its contents. I am taken aback by her newfound respect for my privacy. I carefully slit open the flap and remove the sheet of paper with the typed statement of results. The horror at what I see has my bladder begging for immediate relief but there is no choice but to share the incriminating contents with the hawk Mother. I scan it over and over again, hoping my eyes have deceived me. But the numbers remain the same.

The reality of my first-year results are a far cry from the glories that saw me adorn the front page of the *EP Herald* the year before. I take an instinctive step back and clear my throat.

"Did you pass?" Her bark demands an answer. I take a deep inhale.

"Well, I passed most of my subjects very well. I missed some of the main law courses but that's because many of the lecturers are foreign nationals whose accents baffle me." I am amazed how easily that came out.

The inescapable reality is, however, that I have failed all my law courses. Even worse is that I have missed the supplementary rewrites by a few marks in each. The truth is that this is all my fault. I have spent little to no time in class, at the library or in my room preparing for lectures, tests and even exams.

Drinking and friends have been my downfall. I read the end of the letter. UCT will permit me to return provided I register in any other faculty. Studying law is out the window. I can't bring myself to look at the woman who sits on the floor, legs stretched out in front. Her dagger eyes give me the silent treatment. The unspoken code is "You may walk within ten metres of me but do so at your peril for I will use whatever is in my reach to bludgeon you to death."

I slowly back out of the room, carefully placing my death proclamation on the cabinet to my right. The reality of this disaster is that I am more disappointed in myself than she could ever be. I have never failed a single subject in my life and less than a year ago I emerged among the top performers in my grade. Until now I have had no idea what academic failure is like.

Heart beating in terror at what punishment awaits me, I plunge myself into making supper. I take great care to prepare specific dishes that are The Mother's favourites in the hope that I will be spared her sinister silent treatment. When The Father returns from work my bowels churn in agony at the thought of his size-twelve shoe.

Nothing happens. The silent treatment from The Mother continues, but to my surprise The Father is exceptionally pleasant. As days go by, I resign myself to the humiliation of a failed first attempt at liberty. The irony doesn't escape me that I am no better than Tando and his tail-between-the legs failure. When the registration dates for the following year loom closer, The Father corners me in the kitchen one afternoon while I am doing dishes.

"Your mother and I have had a discussion about your results. She feels that if we remove you from UCT, you will be left demoralised, so we have decided that you should return and try again in a different faculty."

I stare at him. I can't help but think that this has "I finally stood up to your mother and told her where to get off" written all over it. I look into his eyes, fountains of gratitude shining in my own, and thank him. A few moments after he has retreated to the lounge, The Mother enters the kitchen.

"Did Victor tell you what we agreed on with you and UCT?"

"Yes, he did." Although I turn to face her, my head is dropped in 'Do not test The Mother' mode.

"Well, I guess tomorrow you can go to Greenacres to book a bus for your return to Cape Town."

Before I can thank her she has disappeared into the hallway, back to her Bible and bedroom. I stand for a moment gobsmacked at how the winds have tilted the sails in my favour. But I don't spend too long wondering how The Parents have suddenly had this compassionate change of heart, perhaps the first and only one I have ever experienced from them. I am too full of joy at the realisation that I have managed to dodge a major bullet and, in so doing, I am getting another shot at the life I so badly crave.

FIFTEEN

A Year Later

"It's for you."

I hesitantly walk the two steps from where I have been sitting and take the phone from my six-year-old niece. It's a year later, the end of my second year at UCT, and I am back home, but not in PE. I am back in my real home, Mthatha. I have recently removed the white bandage from my left wrist.

I glance at my aged grandmother, who sits daintily next to the phone, eyes transfixed on the TV. I wedge myself between her armrest and the window, catching a glimpse of the giant Christmas tree that adorns part of the front yard.

"Hello?'

The familiar grate of that voice catches me unaware.

"Listen here, you are no longer my child. Do you hear me! I do not want to see you again – you were never a Mabenge to begin with."

"Okay, thank you." My words come out on autopilot.

I replace the receiver and return to my slouching position. How did she know I was here? Who has betrayed me, lied to me that I would find solace here?

My grandmother breaks my discorded thoughts.

"Who was that?"

"Your bully of a child, Tilili."

"What did she want from you?" Her voice is gentle.

"To tell me that I am no longer her child, and that I was never a Mabenge."

To my immediate left sits my grandfather; he says nothing. I wait for someone to say something, anything. But ... nothing.

I stand up and walk out to the kitchen. I find my aunt, my Ma, sitting on a small chair in front of my grandmother's prized Welcome Dover stove. A fire crackles in the grate. She too says nothing. I pull up a second chair beside her and silently embrace the melancholic percussions of the fire that warms us from behind. With no words to share, I peel back my left jacket sleeve to reveal the still raw tracks, the cuts that were intended to end my life. Ma looks away.

My mind returns to that night, a few weeks previously.

○

From the moment I return to varsity after the December break in PE to restart my studies, this time registering for a BCom, the pace and demands on me feel unmanageable. I am overcome with anxiety much of the time, my heart in spasm, my nerves on edge. Instead of honouring my studies, I retreat to my bed and sleep. If I'm not sleeping, I'm crouched on the floor behind the door of my one-bedroomed bachelor flat. Despite being elected to the residence house committee the previous year, it's not enough to save me from my wretched life.

Almost nine months have passed and I have achieved nothing. I close my eyes and bring my knees up to meet my chest. When was the last time I had a proper meal? Maybe last week ... or was it the week before? I feel utterly alone. She was right, The Mother. Her words won't stop tormenting me. "You are nothing. You're a whore. You're a failure." She has always been right. I am so thirsty. I drag myself up from the floor and into the tiny kitchen. The cupboards are as empty as my heart. I take the only glass I have, pour myself water and gulp it down. For a moment it stills the pangs of hunger.

I hear a cacophony of voices and loud footsteps outside. They are like gunshots. Most students are up and about, occupied with the business of what they have come to university to achieve. I am nothing. I am a failure.

I need to do something. I move to the front door. I catch sight of the slightly protruding cyan vein on my left wrist as my hand touches the door handle. I hear Thandi opening her door, probably returning from lectures. We now stay on the same floor in single bachelor flats. With a heavy sigh, I turn the lever down, pulling the door towards me. I move my left foot, in an ancient Island Style black sandal that has seen better days, one step forward. My right one follows. The late afternoon meets me as I shuffle out my door into the corridor. The remnants of the sun gleam above the corrugated tops of Liesbeeck Gardens. Everything looks like it's dying. I greet Thandi with a frozen, half-hearted smile.

"Where you been, chommie? I've been looking for you the entire day."

"Studying in my room." The lie slips from my lips.

"When last did you eat, Mabenge? Have your parents still not sent you money for food?"

"They did, chommie … I ate earlier today." Another lie.

Thandi gazes into my eyes, piercing through their depth and into my soul.

"Chommie, I know you – you haven't eaten. I can tell."

Thandi and I have grown closer over the months; she is just about the only person I ever talk to. She fills the void when The Parents neglect to send me funds, sometimes for weeks on end, depending on their moods.

She stops herself mid-motion of locking her door and opens it again.

"Come inside, chommie. Let me make you something to eat."

Hunger gets the better of shame. With my head hung, I sheepishly follow her into her flat. My mind is lost in dark and anxious thoughts as Thandi prepares a meal. I have reached deep rock bottom. I can no longer allow myself the humiliation of a leppered Lazarus. I scan her shelves, looking for a sign, something that will assist me in my longing for release. I try to stay in the taupe armchair close to her desk, across from her bed, and nod as she makes conversation me. But I am too deep in a pit of pity and shame. I long for silence. I am undeserving of this life.

A while later Thandi hands me a plate of golden brown chicken and fluffy rice. My eyes are unable meet hers; my lips try to mumble "thanks" but stay stiff and frozen. I begin to dig in. I try to disguise my hunger by forcing myself to slow down. I am starving. Each mouthful reminds me that I do not remember when last I have eaten. With the last forkful in my mouth, I raise my head to meet Thandi's eyes. They are warm and sympathetic. I read her expression as pity. Oh god, I can't do this any more. She picks up the plate and returns to the kitchen to do the dishes. I am on my feet, following her.

"No, chommie, that is the least I can do to thank you. This was amazing." I find my voice and grab the plate.

I place the dishes in the sink, squirt some liquid dishwashing soap and warm water onto them. I begin washing each plate diligently, but my eye is fixed on the pulsating cyan vein in my left wrist. It beats in time to the voice in my head: "You're not good enough. You will never amount to anything."

Through the tiny kitchen window overlooking the courtyard, I see the onset of evening. The darkness looms. I walk away from the sink and pause in the hallway, staring into Thandi's open bathroom. A gigantic pair of orange-headed scissors on the windowsill beckons me.

"Chommie, can I quickly use your bathroom?"

It is not a request but a statement. I quietly close the door behind me. I stare at a stranger's face in the mirror. Without a thought, as though I am on autopilot, I pick up the scissors with my right hand and clench my teeth. My heart thuds. I glide the scissor blade back and forth against the vein in my wrist. A tiny moment of lucidity brings me back to the bathroom. My mind lurches back to my child self. The day I was beaten until I shat myself. The days of hunger, the nights going to bed having had nothing but water. The names: "whore" ... "Aids-infested loser". I look deeply into the mirror and all I see is the little person forced into the mechanics of being a girl, when they truly feel they are a boy.

A river of tears stream down my face as I bid my life farewell. I open the tap and take the scissors into my right hand again. I place my thumb into the smaller of its two heads and the rest of my fingers into its larger enclosure. I open the blades wide and place my left wrist down on the cold enamel washbasin. I hold it between the blades, and began slicing with vigour. All the while her voice plays itself over and over in my head: "You will never amount to anything." I savage my flesh with the blades not sharp enough; the pain is immeasurable. I eventually manage to saw enough to tear through a thin layer of fat to expose the vein, and a river of red blood beckons me to release it. Deeper. I keep slicing. The river soon becomes a flood. I need to get the blades around the vein and snip right through. As I ravage my wrist, gaining momentum through the dulled motivating pain, the door opens and in walks Thandi. The scissors fall. She screams. I collapse onto the blood-soaked floor. I slip into nothing. And to nothing I will return.

SIXTEEN

Birgit

I haven't seen Birgit Schreiber, my therapist on campus, for at least a month in the weeks leading up to me gouging my wrist. Instead I've been holed up in my flat. Not going to lectures. Not going to therapy. I've literally disappeared. AWOLed from everything and everyone.

I first meet Birgit early in 2001, a few weeks into my second year at UCT, now a first-year BCom student.

Almost immediately into the new academic year I sense that I'm not coping. The rose-tinted feelings of being allowed by The Parents to study again soon evaporate and within a month of being back in Cape Town, my coffers run empty. My residence status has moved to self-catering – The Parents are fully aware that they need to provide me with a monthly stipend for groceries, but my calls to them go unanswered and soon thereafter Tando informs me that it would be in my best interests to stop calling them. But I am no longer shocked by the irrational and cruel actions of these two people.

A week goes by without eating. I am forced to call my grandmother in Mthatha to get funds for food and toiletries. She manages to send me R150, which I have to stretch for the month. Sometimes she can't help and then I am forced to hound Tando until he makes a plan to send me something.

My desperation grows like aggressive cancer. I don't sleep. I am in a constant state of panic. Deeply depressed, I struggle to leave my room, skipping classes and tutorials because I am far too tired and too hungry to move.

The frustrated boy inside me, the one I have tried to shelve away in my mental archives, now announces his presence as each day goes by. By now I've completely stopped wearing women's clothes and have retreated into the lonely pockets of a nomadic existence. My gut keeps telling me that I need help, that I need to do something, to speak to someone. Locked up alone in my room, the only person to converse with is myself. My ramblings often dissolve into hallucinations.

In the first few months I somehow still manage to submit my assignments and essays and even write tests because I need to ensure I get a DP clearance to write exams. I have been readily accepted into the Commerce faculty and, though I detest accounting, I have been assigned Accounting as a major by the course convener who does not understand what "someone who had got ninety per cent for matric Accounting wanted to do in the law faculty in the first place".

On an afternoon that I do manage to leave my room, I take a walk from Upper to Lower Campus after submitting an assignment. When I get to the buildings that house the student health division I impulsively decide to walk inside and pick up a brochure about the mental health services on offer. At the front desk I am shown to the adjacent building that houses the resident psychologists, psychiatrists and student counsellors. I am greeted by a jovial receptionist who asks me to fill in a form and wait while she finds someone who can assess my need. As I fill in forms, I wonder whether I should make a dash for it. I'm not sure what has come over me. It is very uncharacteristic of me to seek help and even worse is the possibility that these therapists might disclose what I share with them to The Parents who will surely murder me.

Suddenly a door to my right opens and a serious-looking white woman, clad in a floral power blouse and skirt, emerges. She walks straight to me and asks me to accompany her into her office.

The woman introduces herself as Birgit Schreiber, a psychologist who's been assigned to my case. There is something about her eyes that makes me feel safe. After she's done with the introductions, she asks why I've decided to pay the facility a visit this particular afternoon.

What shall I tell her? What do I say? My mind stutters in panic. How do I even start to explain to her the life I have been trying to manage? So I spin her a story about not being able to cope academically despite the endless effort I put into my work. We touch on other aspects of my life, including family history, relations with peers and dating life. But I am a closed door; I reveal very little. At the end of the hour, Birgit suggests that we meet once a week for the following few weeks so that she can properly assess my needs. I hesitantly agree, battling to maintain any kind of eye contact with her.

I open up a little more on my next visit. We begin delving into my childhood. I revisit a time of joy as I eagerly describe my early years in the dusty streets of Ncambedlana. I speak fondly of my grandparents and the aunt who raises me as her own, the one I believed for so long was my mother. When I get to the part where the rug is pulled from under my feet and I am removed from Umtata to live with The Parents in PE, I freeze.

Birgit allows me to pause for reflection. When I look into her soft, empathetic eyes, I feel safe enough for the chains that have been holding the entanglements of my truth and pain to be broken. Slowly, in a monotonous voice, I start to tell her of the life I have lived under the control of The Parents. Halfway through, Birgit stops me.

"The way in which you're telling your story sounds like a recording ... I still have no idea how you're really *feeling*."

For a moment I want to retreat back into my shell. But I know that if I don't allow this woman in now, I will continue to live in hell, in this veiled existence. My alter ego keeps wanting to surface and announce himself and reveal the true dynamics that plague the disequilibrium between my being and the body in which I have been born. But I have not established a strong-enough relationship with Birgit yet, and don't feel safe enough to allow "him" a platform just yet.

"I'm not sure I understand what you mean," I lie. "I am telling you everything that happened to me over the last few years."

"I want you to tell me how what happened to you made you *feel* and what it makes you feel right now."

This woman is trying to draw emotions from me I'm not sure I want to deal with. The Mother has put the fear of God in me about ever telling what truly happened behind closed doors. Hell, she has even gone as far as threatening me with death if I dare talk about her to other people. I sit frozen, listening to the voices in my head and imagining the risks involved in letting this person in.

"Yolanda," says Birgit, "we have to try."

I look into Birgit's eyes for a very long time and finally, heart pounding, make a decision to trust this complete stranger with the life I have lived and somehow survived.

It is as though a plug in the cement of my being has been released. Slowly I begin writing my feelings down in essays that I submit weekly. I begin noticing small signs of affection in the way Birgit shakes my hand before ushering me into her office or briefly pats me on the back as I walk out after each encounter.

Talking to her helps me prepare for the June exams. But when the semester ends and the university closes, I find myself thrust back into the darkness of my world. For a while there will be no weekly sessions with Birgit. Most of my friends and house residents have left for the holidays, and I find myself scavenging the streets of Mowbray and Rondebosch looking for the next pint of lager, with the sole goal of drowning the sorrows and dark voices that threaten to suffocate me.

Despite working hard, my results are below par. I am anxious to resume my sessions with Birgit when the new term starts. She immediately notices my increased levels of anxiety and unease.

She suggests a time out from my academic commitments, which she will motivate in full to my faculty. But I reassure her that I have never needed time out before and am fine to continue the year as I still have six months to recover the points I need in order to pass the year. But of course I am not coping. I soon find myself spending many late nights and early evenings perched on

Liesbeeck's rooftop, with a half-empty wine bottle in one hand and a deep urge to jump and end this life. I begin reaching out to Birgit from rooftops. Many evenings are spent talking to her as my feet peep over a ledge.

I find myself begging her to give me reasons why I should not just jump and end it all. Her concerned voice, always so accepting of me, echoes through the phone and assures me that I have a lot to offer the world. We speak until I allow her to convince me to sit down, take a couple of breaths and remember that our next session is just around the corner.

Then The Mother, who has been silent for a while, suddenly makes her serpentine appearance and begins taunting me with a string of harassing phone calls. I withdraw from everybody, especially Thandi, who has been my confidante and pillar of support, helping me with groceries and food whenever she notices that I have none. I even begin avoiding Birgit and therapy, as it has been getting increasingly draining and leaving me with feelings of being broken beyond repair.

As the year draws to its end, my days have become so dark that I see no light or possible way to dig myself out. I allow my alter ego more airplay, and it reminds me that no one will ever accept me as a man in a woman's body. I spend night after night awake, not able to sleep, sitting on the balcony gazing into the dark night sky, talking to a God I believe to be evil. I ask Him not for serenity but for courage to end my life.

SEVENTEEN

No Answers

The crackling and spluttering of flames bring me back to the kitchen in Mthatha with Ma. I am deep in thought, thinking about the call from The Mother in which she disowned me. Her sister sits resigned beside me.

"Ma, how did your flesh and blood – Nokuzola – go so wrong?"

She has no answer.

"Tomorrow we will have to refill your prescription for antidepressants and sleeping pills." Ma's voice is warm and gentle.

"Why is no one standing up to her?" I glare into her eyes, mine flashing with rage. "Are you telling me that all of you are too scared of her? What happened to her to make her so evil?"

Ma thinks for a long time.

"I cannot say for certain. What I do know is that Sis Nokuzola has always been an angry person. Perhaps her divorce from her first husband left her bitter and vengeful."

My grandfather walks into the kitchen and sits down in his usual spot between the cabinet and breakfast table. I refuse to let up on the conversation, aware that I am moving into untapped territory, but I want to evoke some form of response from him.

Until I had met Birgit, my voice had been silenced. Throughout my life I have been socialised into submission and taught that, as a child, I am always wrong no matter what the elder has done. Well, to hell with that. Tonight someone is going to give me answers.

"I can understand that, but what does her divorce have to do with me? She just called me now to tell me I was never a Mabenge and that she disowns me ... and I believe her."

I catch a wave of grief pass across Ma's already drained and hollow eyes. She stands up, walks the few steps towards the sink and places her empty coffee mug down. The years have aged her. She has lost a considerable amount of weight and the mauve caftan she once filled out now hangs loosely on her skeleton frame. She opens the tap, rinses her mug and places it on the drying tray. Then she lifts her head and gazes out the tiny kitchen window into the darkness in front of her. I am frustrated by her avoidance of my question. I glance at my grandfather who too is lost in an empty stare. I focus on him for a while, hoping the heaviness of my glare will lure his eyes to mine and offer some answers. Ma finally breaks the silence.

"My sister was once the leading lady of our quaint Ncambedlana Community. She had all the talents to cement her position as the firstborn. She could sing, she was gifted academically and she had an amazing way with words."

I switch off at "leading lady". I am not interested in hearing how she once was. What matters to me is how she currently is and how she has managed to wield her cruelty over me to a point where I believe my destiny is tied to death and failure.

"Why is everyone trying to justify what could have gone wrong? No one seems to understand that this woman has been terrorising some of her children for years. No one has ever done anything about that."

Ma sighs heavily. "I'll be honest with you ... We had some idea of what you might be going through, but it was never our place to intervene. Your parents were married and so, to avoid meddling in matrimonial affairs, we left it to your paternal family to interject."

I am outraged. "Well, I can tell you now, not a single one of them ever did step forward. Instead, they watched us suffer and chose to ignore our pain every time."

I am extremely anxious about bashing Ma with words like this, but I have got to a point where I need answers and she is the gateway to fulfilling that need. My grandmother shuffles in and demands that we stop refuelling the fire and make sure it has died completely before we retire to bed. I roll my eyes and continue.

"You cannot begin to imagine the horrors Tando and I had to endure, Ma … And now you expect me to believe that not a single person could stand up to her."

The silence eats up the room.

My grandfather's voice finally ends it.

"I do not know what happened to my child Nokuzola. I really cannot tell you why she became the person she is."

He tries hard to swallow his tears. I have never seen my grandfather so vulnerable. He is breathing heavily and I worry that his eighty-six-year-old heart might not be able to handle the pressure I have put on him by demanding answers.

But I can't stop myself. "I feel something more should have been done, especially after she spouted all those profanities about all of you when I went to live with her. Surely that should have been an indication of what was truly going on with her? Even the way she tried to remove me the first time. I would've thought you would have provided me and Tando with more support."

I am at full tilt now. My heart is racing and the hairs on my back stand to attention. I need to get all of my rage out if I have any hope of healing. When I look at my grandfather again his head hangs in shame. It's a look that reminds me of my own demeanour after being reprimanded or even beaten by The Parents. Submission runs in the family. The grey on his head tugs at my heart strings and I immediately hate myself.

"In the same breath," I try to soften the blow I have already dealt him, "I do feel you and Miss K did the best you could have done as parents. None of your other children turned out evil. Instead, I am back here in my home being healed by this family. So maybe we should accept that we will never know the source of her resentment and cruelty … Perhaps it's just time to move on."

With that, I stand up and walk out of the tiny kitchen. Ma follows me. Soon we are lying next to each other, in the same bed we shared all those years ago. But I find no peace in sleep.

EIGHTEEN

Stitched Up

After collapsing in a pool of blood on Thandi's bathroom floor, I remember nothing. I am jerked back to life by the sharp tang of ammonia a nurse holds to my nose. The first question the trauma doctor asks me as I struggle into consciousness is whether I am on private medical aid. I look at the medical team in white coats floating around me and wonder if I'm in heaven surrounded by a choir of angels. When it finally dawns on me that I'm in a hospital, I respond with a counter question.

"Where am I?"

A nurse, clearly annoyed, responds that I am at the Vincent Pallotti in Pinelands.

"Are you on private medical aid?" She repeats the doctor's question. "If you aren't, we cannot treat you here," she snarls.

I am, I tell them. The army general, who's in fact the head matron, leaves my side for a moment and I am now attended to by a younger nurse who informs me that we have to await approval from the scheme before they can administer any medication or attend to the wound on my wrist.

I am unable to muster the courage to look at the fruits of my failed attempt. When Matron Stalin returns with the doctor, I am informed that, according to the details I have provided, I am no longer a member of my parents' medical aid. The only dependants cited are my younger siblings and I am asked to confirm their names, which I do. With that, I am told that a call has been made to Groote Schuur Hospital, where I will be treated, stitched and, if necessary, referred to the psychiatric unit for observation.

Within an hour I am wheeled into the Groote Schuur trauma unit and carted off to an admissions holding area for initial observation. I have heard many disturbing stories about this hospital. I scan my new surroundings. Depression lingers in the air and the blood-stained tiles confirm the stark difference between private-sector and public healthcare.

A tall young white man dressed in scrubs walks over to me and introduces himself as an intern. He asks me to fill in admission forms and proceeds to prep a medical tray with stitching equipment. I panic when I get to *Next of Kin* on the form. I cannot bring myself to fill in The Parents' details, so I submit my grandmother's particulars. With my administration complete, the young man proceeds to stitch my wrist. Only then do I find the courage to steal a look at the results of my pathetic attempt at suicide. I see remnants of my crusty blood flaked across my hand and wrist. The flesh around the wound is tinted a sickly shade of green. I watch the intern's attempts at stitching me up as he tries to distract me by way of arbitrary conversation around my life's ambitions and career goals. When he has sewn my wound closed and realises I am in no mood for his undercover investigation, he summons the porter to escort me to the ward where the doctors will decide what should happen next. The clock on the wall indicates ten minutes after midnight.

I must have dosed off shortly after as I'm suddenly woken by a doctor calling my name and instructing me to sit up. I check the time again. It's 6am. He advises me he'll be sending a porter to accompany me to the psychiatric unit where I will undergo a full evaluation to decide whether they can discharge me. With that, the doctor turns and leaves just as breakfast is wheeled in: sloppy oats and a slice of toast with peanut butter. I need to find the ablution area.

As I wander through the desolate ward, my alter ego emerges

and plants an idea in my head. With no security in sight I can easily pull down the sleeve of my jacket and walk out without alerting anyone. I sit in the closed lavatory, my head hanging between my legs, trying to erase the notion. I stand up and pace around the toilet area, but just as I've convinced myself to make a dash for it, a nurse walks in and shuffles me back to my assigned bed.

Soon I am wheeled to the psych unit. I am buzzed into a temporary holding facility and formally booked into the system as a psychiatric patient. My right arm is tagged and I am released into the general waiting area with other patients due to be evaluated. I watch transfixed as patients engage in conversations with themselves, occasionally laughing out loud at nothing in particular. This convinces me that, because I'm nothing like these crazies, I'll surely be eligible for discharge.

I'm finally called into the doctor's office. We begin our conversation with the usual prying into my childhood and background. I narrate most of what I have already shared with Birgit. As I babble on about The Parents and their selective brutality he stops me mid-sentence.

"Why do you keep going back to your parents?"

I am floored. I cannot answer. The pain in my wrist throbs.

"It seems to me that you have one family that cares about you deeply. The way you speak about your maternal family makes me wonder why you don't go back to them."

"It's not that easy, Doctor. I can't just decide to go back to Mthatha without The Parents' consent."

His response hits hard.

"From what you have told me, your parents will never give you consent. You need to make that decision by yourself and for yourself."

I slump deeper into the soiled armchair. He makes it sound so easy. The memory of my eleven-year-old self flashes into my mind, the child who tried to run away and was instead captured and beaten to a pulp. The same family he is urging me to return to has been aware of my plight all along. Hell, they had even sent Ma to check up on me and, instead of removing me, she had told me there was nothing she could do for me. How then would I be able to trust that they would not do the same again? What guarantee did I have that they would not ship me back to The Parents?

"Like I told you, I have tried running away before … It did not work."

"This time you will not be running away. This time you will be returning to Mthatha. Remember, within a few months you are going to be twenty-one and you will no longer require parental consent to do anything."

This man makes sense. None of what he has said is new to me but it's the way in which he says it, so sensible, logical, and convinces me to consider the broader picture. My alter ego interrupts my thoughts, and nudges me to tell him how I truly feel about being a twenty-year-old lost in a body in which I do not belong. I silence the notion faster than the speed of a shooting star. I am making progress with this gentleman and will see the outside of these walls sooner if I keep that part of me concealed.

"I am going to make a call to student counselling services and speak to your psychologist. I cannot release you unless it is into her care."

My silly, naive heart does somersaults as I assume he means I'll be moving in with Birgit and her boyfriend. Maybe she will really take care of me, adopt me, so I need never return to The Parents. It is only after he returns from his chat with Birgit that I realise what it all really means.

"Ms Schreiber has agreed to arrange for you to be admitted into a wellness programme at Kenilworth Clinic. She's going to send a shuttle to pick you up and take you to the facility. When you get to your residence, please make sure you turn your phone on so that she is able to reach you."

He has given me a lot of food for thought and if I am going to have a shot at this game called life I have to give myself a chance. The porter returns to wheel me downstairs and leaves a security guard with strict instructions to make sure I stay put and wait for my shuttle.

When I arrive at Liesbeeck Gardens to pick up my things there is no welcoming party. I knock on the warden's door and, with a look that screams, "Shame, this poor child who has abandonment issues," she ushers me in and leads me to her lounge area where she asks me to take a seat.

"I called your parents last night after you'd been rushed to hospital."

I want to die the minute I realise the pace at which my situation has escalated. Beads of sweat begin to form on my forehead, my neck, down my back, prompting me to remove my sweater as I try to regain my composure and still my panicked breathing.

"I'm sorry to have to tell you this but I have to be brutally honest with you. Your mother told me that you're an attention seeker and that we should have you locked up in the mental asylum."

I lift my eyes to meet hers, tears threatening to burst from their ducts. I'm not sure her revelation warrants a response.

"I've spoken to your psychologist as well, and she informs me you'll be going to Kenilworth Clinic for some time. Is there anyone else we can contact on the home front? Your father's family, your grandparents?"

"We can call my grandparents in Mthatha." I write down the number, hiding my left wrist.

"We'll make contact with them sometime today. In the meantime, please go to your room and pack some clothes while we wait for Birgit to arrange for your admission to the clinic."

I creep past Thandi's door, ashamed of ever showing my face again. But she must hear me slip the key into my lock because within seconds her door has swung open and she has me enveloped in her arms, making me promise never to scare her like that again. We step into my flat; I try to avoid eye contact. The conversation, propelled by her, gets straight to the point: what now?

"Chommie, we know your parents are not going to save you. We know they are the sole reason you find yourself where you are now. Mabenge, you are not some skeleton that must live a second-class existence because of the brutality of your childhood. Chommie, I think it's time you make the decision to go back to your grandparents. To Mthatha."

"I don't think that's a good idea. My parents will kill me."

"Mabenge! At this point your parents do not care whether you live or die. So maybe we need to accept that, to them, you are already dead. Go home, Mabenge – and home is Mthatha."

Her point is made. The only time Thandi uses my surname is when she needs to hammer some sense into me. We sit in silence before my phone rings. It's Birgit; she is clearly deeply concerned. She quickly informs me of what my next steps should be. Thandi helps me pack what little I have into my high-school tog bag and we sit in silence, waiting for the arrival of the shuttle that will ferry me to Kenilworth. When it arrives, we walk in silence down to the ground floor where she hugs me, giving the driver stern instructions to deliver me safely at my destination. My eyes fill with tears of gratitude for Thandi who never tires of trying to unpack my childhood with me, to understand the demons that drive The Parents. In my darkest moments, she calls me back by telling me that I am amazing, that I am destined for great things and that I matter to her.

NINETEEN

Homeward Bound

As the driver pulls slowly into the drive at the clinic, I spot Birgit waiting for me. I can read the sadness in her eyes as she steps forward to take me in her arms.

"I've booked you in here for two weeks," she explains. "You're a very bright young person. Use this time to find healing." She takes my hand, gently squeezing it.

I spend the next fortnight unpacking my pain and wounds with other people to whom life has also been unkind. Some are battling addiction and many are suffering the abandonment of families and communities. It is here that I come to realise that I am not alone, that many of us walk around shouldering invisible crosses that weigh heavily on us, requiring us to find ways to carry them as best we can. For the first time in my life I am not profiled according to gender and I begin trusting these strangers with parts of myself I have not even spoken to Birgit about. My alter ego intensifies efforts to get me to open up about who I really am, what I truly feel and who I am attracted to in my daily life. We meditate, we cry, we sit in silence. I start to feel alive for the first time since I was eleven. I embrace my newfound sanctuary, lapping up each word of encouragement to live, to be and to matter.

Two weeks fly by. When my final day draws to a close I hold onto Sonia, the matron, for dear life. She has become like a mother to me. She cups my face in her hands and tells me to look into her eyes.

"There is so much you have to offer the world. Take it one day at a time. My hope for you is that whatever you decide to be, whoever you are attracted to and wherever you find love, remember the power that lies within you."

I have never been held or spoken to so intimately before. In all the years in PE, The Mother never stroked me or hugged me.

I leave Kenilworth Clinic with newfound purpose. I feel like I have been given a torch to find my way through the darkness and heal, become the person I am destined to be.

When I return to Liesbeeck Gardens I make my way to the warden's house. She seems happy to see me.

"You're looking much better. We spoke to your family in Mthatha and they have booked a bus for you. You will be going home tomorrow evening."

I am filled with joy. I am going home. Home! I try to quell the unease when my mind darts to The Parents. The warden informs me that neither of them have called to enquire about me or my health. Thandi's words, "You are dead to them," ring true. I march off to my room with my head held high.

The following morning I brave the prying eyes of fellow res mates; I am convinced everyone knows about my left wrist. I take a shuttle to Lower Campus. I had been advised by the warden to stop by Birgit's office at 9am before I make final preparations for my trip to Mthatha. The smile on Birgit's face reminds me of the warmth of the sun on a bright summer morning. She ushers me in and offers me a glass of water. She's consulted with the clinical psychiatrist at Kenilworth Clinic who has told her that I've been put on a treatment course of antidepressants and sleeping pills, to help me with my healing. In addition, she has written to my faculty head and advised her that I need a period of six months away from my academic commitments in order to recuperate and regain the strength I need to continue with my education. This in effect means that I will not be returning to UCT until the second semester of the following year. I have grown to trust Birgit and believe that any decision she takes concerning me is in my best interests.

"There's something I need to tell you, but I am scared that it will change the way in which you see me." I gather courage to speak my truth.

Birgit's smile encourages me to continue.

"I like girls and I've always wondered if I was meant to be born a boy."

There, I've said it.

Brigit's smile remains. It's as though I have told her I like ham and not cheese, no knee-jerk reaction, no judgement. Instead she tells me that sexual attraction between people of the same gender is completely normal. I interject, hoping she will understand what I am truly trying to tell her.

"But I have always felt like I am a boy who is in a girl's body. I know this sounds absurd and even I battle to reconcile it in my mind."

She pauses to reflect for a moment before responding.

"Let's take this one journey at a time. Right now you are dealing with abandonment and abuse issues from your childhood and part of your adulthood. I think we need to focus on that element of your healing first, then we can look into the dynamics of your feelings around your attraction towards other people."

I sigh but agree to her plan of action. I had hoped she would whip out one of her gigantic psychology textbooks and give me a scientific explanation and give me a name, a diagnosis for feeling the way I do. Before I leave her office, she urges me to continue taking my medication and to use the time in Mthatha to reconnect with my grandparents and the woman I have always loved as my mother, Ma.

I walk back to res, a surge of energy in my heart. I am going home to Ncambedlana, Mthatha.

☽

I'm jolted from sleep as the Greyhound bus driver announces that we are making a stop in Port Elizabeth. My heart shoots through the roof. What if someone has alerted The Mother that I'm on the bus, and she's waiting at Greenacres, guns blazing, planning to violently remove me? I wedge myself deeper into the upper-level window seat and say a silent prayer. When we eventually pull into the station, I snuggle myself under my travel blanket and glue my eyes to my phone. It seems like forever before the last passenger has been loaded and the doors slide shut. Of course The Mother has no idea that I am on the bus, a stone's throw from her house of hell, but this is how intensely I fear her. She does not even have to be in the same room to trigger such a reaction in me. This terror has been ingrained in my DNA since the age of eleven.

I exhale, and breathe easier as the bus winds its way briskly across the hilly plains, taking me back to a world I left behind all those years ago. I notice with glee the infamous Kei Bridge that once served as the boundary between the Transkei and old apartheid South Africa. As if on cue, the density of the subtropical climate ushers in the aromatic scent of fynbos, which filters through the overhead vents, leaving a lingering familiar smell, fuelling the excitement building up inside me.

The bus pulls up in Mthatha just before sunset. And before I know it, I step over the threshold to find Ma sitting on a small stool behind the kitchen door. She lifts her eyes to meet mine and for a moment we lock into each other, reconnected by love, by the bond that has been severed too soon. She leaps to her feet, embracing me, dissolving into tears of joy. It's been seven years since we held each other.

TWENTY

Healing in Mthatha

The Mother's decision to disown me frees me. The healing that started at the clinic continues in Mthatha. Slowly. Each morning I wake up slightly groggy and try to reflect on everything that's happened to bring me to this place. I have been prescribed a bag of antidepressants and sleeping pills and am aware of a dull film that settles over my mind. I hope that beneath their pearly coating the pills will perform some miracle on my state of mind.

I wonder if I'm at that place people refer to as "rock bottom". I try to focus on my immediate surroundings. So many things have changed in this maze. My grandparents have aged; Ma is no longer working and has developed a very close relationship with Gordon's London Dry Gin.

Time creeps along, prompting me to spend more and more time under the bedcovers, believing that this is part of the journey to healing. But by the time Christmas comes, it feels like I am deteriorating. I have barely enough energy to climb out of bed, let alone find myself back in the rhythm of chores and activity in the home. I spend more and more time locked away in my mind. I realise that I have reached a point of feeling enormous loss. I have been so eager to abandon The Parents that it dawns on me one day that I have no tools to live outside of the terror they have instilled in me. Until now, they have been the voices I have listened to, drumming in my inadequacies and failures. Now that they have been removed from the equation, I have nothing but a big empty hole inside me.

I sink deeper into depression. I manage to shelve my alter ego, hide it deep in the fissures of my mind. At this point I can hardly get out of bed, let alone try to deal with the idea that I'm attracted to women or find myself in the wrong body.

Over time my grandmother becomes increasingly annoyed with my bedridden existence. She takes it upon herself to wake me every morning after the rest of the household has left for work. We spend time together listening to radio Umhlobo Wenene and tending to her garden. Her routine has not changed much over the years. Helped along by three cups of her delicious Mona brew, she still manages a thriving organic set-up that includes tending to chicken, ducks, vegetables and a variety of fruit.

One afternoon, as we sit in the shade of my grandfather's prized pine tree, I brave myself to subtly enquire about the woman who birthed me.

"Miss K, what do you think happened to this firstborn daughter of yours? What was she like as a child?"

"Why are you asking me these questions? Did Mzalwane not give you a satisfactory answer? These are questions you should be asking him about his child."

My grandmother has always had a way of handing difficult issues to my grandfather. As a result, she has not uttered a single word about her daughter since the evening The Mother called to disown me.

Finally she manages a single line. "I do not know what is wrong with her."

I sit gobsmacked. Surely this grandmother is not serious. How can she not know her own child? I do not blame her for the evil of her child; all I want is an explanation of how the child who came from her womb can be so disingenuous, so different from all her other children. I press on.

"Is there anything you might have done as a parent that could have turned her into the person she is?"

No response. My grandmother lifts her head, turning it in the direction of her rose garden, mumbling something about needing a new set of pruning shears. A sharp anger begins brewing inside of me. It builds until I can take it no more.

"What type of mother gives birth to six children and only loves two? How sick must this child of yours be to continue popping children who she ends up giving away before returning to violently remove them and torture them in ways I cannot even begin to describe? You are just as responsible as she is for not telling me the truth."

With that I struggle to my feet, the rage seething in me almost tripping me up as I storm off, pulling out a packet of cigarettes and puffing my lungs away. I am livid. I smoke three sticks before making my way back into the yard to find my grandmother no longer seated under the tree where I left her. We continue the rest of the day in silence and when we do resume talking again, no mention is made of our earlier altercation.

It is only months later, when I refuse to return to UCT, that we again broach the subject of the evil that is The Mother. Finally, my grandmother speaks. She is fully aware of the cruelty of The Mother but, much as she would like to, she cannot disown her own daughter. She understands my anger but begs me not to become like The Mother.

When I ask her why they – the family, my family – did nothing to help me and Tando as children, she reveals that The Mother had threatened them with legal action if they ever interfered in family relations or with her marriage to The Father, one that never saw any formalities in terms of the traditional rites of lobola. Although this confession leaves me even more confused, a piece of Miss K's advice resonates with me. My genetic construction means that I must have facets of The Mother within me, and if I have any chance of having a shot at this thing called life, then I will have to be careful not to be filled with the same hatred as the person I now so passionately loathe.

A few months into my healing journey I start picking Ma's brain on how we can get Tando back to Mthatha as well. He has heard about my suicide attempt and has kept the lines of communication open by bringing me up to speed about what The Parents are saying about me and the many provocative phone calls The Mother has been making to all her siblings who have chosen to help me. I try to convince my grandparents to bring Tando back to Mthatha by painting a full picture of the reality that both Tando and I suffered during our time in PE, where Tando is still trapped.

When I raise the issue of The Parents' refusal to allow my brother to return to Rhodes and finish his degree, my grandfather is sold. Arrangements are made to wire funds to my brother's bank account and he is soon en route home to complete our little circle.

The difference between Tando and me is that he has never allowed himself to get to tipping point. Where I am entirely asocial here in Mthatha, he gets back home and continues as though he has never left. He rekindles his relationships with friends he has not seen in over a decade and slots himself right back into his previous hood.

As the days draw closer to my varsity departure date, my grandfather – also a clergyman – arranges 'spiritual readiness' sessions with the local Methodist pastor, the Reverend Sigaba. When I raise concerns about using instruments of the Church to deal with human atrocities, my grandfather reminds me that the Church is as human a creation as those atrocities. My initial meeting with the reverend nearly drives me to slit my wrists a second time. She greets me with an affectionate embrace and immediately we speak about my suicide attempt. She asks to see my wrist, which I show her without hesitation. When her curiosity is satisfied, she asks me to look her in the eyes and bluntly tells me that had I succeeded I would never have entered the pearly gates of heaven. I sit just a few feet across from her and feel my anger, which I have worked so hard to tame, awaken.

"If this heaven is the same heaven that has been shoved down my throat by the woman who caused me to sit in front of you today, then I have no interest in it."

With that, I tell her I have a prior engagement, stomp out of her dimly lit office and wait by the gate for my lift to pick me up. I do, however, return the following week, and subsequent sessions are easier. Having failed to convince my grandmother that I no longer want to return to UCT, when the time comes, I say goodbye to my loved ones in Mthatha to return to Cape Town and resume my studies. I leave with a lighter heart.

TWENTY-ONE

Pandora's Box and The Letter

I arrive at the central Cape Town bus station early in the morning and catch a taxi to Mowbray. I'm allocated a new bachelor flat by the warden and, although I am aware of the curious, prying eyes around me, I manage to settle into the swing of student life. I'm sad to discover that my good friend Thandi has switched universities, so I spend most of those first few days back on my own.

When lectures resume the following week, I'm keen to resume therapy with Birgit. We arrange early-morning sessions and instead of being cooped in an office, we go on brisk, often silent walks through the leafy suburb of Rondebosch. I pour my soul into every session, every piece of work I write, and every walk I take with Birgit, who puts equal effort back into my healing. Whenever days are dark and I struggle to make it out the front door, she is always there to will me on towards the light. By the time the year comes to a close, I am clear that I am not at all interested in Accounting as a major. Once again Birgit intervenes and helps me to switch to the triple major stream of Philosophy, Politics and Economics.

When the new academic year starts in 2003, I am far more settled academically. I find philosophy especially intriguing; the readings make me feel that perhaps I'm not such an outcast after all. I join the UCT women's soccer team, which embodies a feeling of masculinity that I long for. Even though none of the women I play with seem to feel attracted to other women like I do, I am encouraged to have brief conversations with women I find beautiful and who are interested in speaking to me.

One afternoon, as I sit in the back seat of the Jammie Shuttle, an older woman whom I have seen from time to time in the passageways of Liesbeeck Gardens takes a seat next to me, even though the shuttle is almost empty. We travel in silence for a long time before she initiates a conversation about the weather. We are soon deep in conversation about other things.

Then she suddenly asks: "I've heard you tried to kill yourself. Why would someone as beautiful as you want to end her life?"

My usual defensiveness shifts to aroused curiosity. I look into her amber eyes and want to know more about her.

"It's a very long story that I don't want to get into now," I offer.

"Maybe you can come by my flat later this evening and we can talk about it." She won't take no for an answer.

"Okay." The minute the word leaves my mouth, my heart hurdles in waves of palpitations. Beads of sweat form on my forehead. My new acquaintance has moved closer and places her hand on my thigh. My toes wiggle; I am filled with that tingling sensation.

When we arrive at Liesbeeck, she waits for me to get off the shuttle. We get into the lift together and when the door opens for her floor, she signals that I should follow her. With a whisper of caution in my heart, I walk slightly behind her, watching her perky bum sway from side to side. She has a certain grace about her. Once inside her flat she invites me into her bedroom and offers me a seat. I nervously thank her, placing my backpack on the floor next to the single-seat lounger, and sit down. She returns with a glass of juice and sits beside me. I muster up enough courage to ask her her name.

"My apologies," she says. "My name is Pandora. I'm originally from a small town in the Eastern Cape."

I like her already. Within no time I'm telling her about my childhood and why I have self-harmed. I'm so comfortable with Pandora that soon I'm confiding in her about my growing attraction towards women, which has recently been dulled somewhat by the medication the clinic has prescribed. Her eyes remain fixed on mine throughout. Then she smiles at me and tells me that she really likes me.

"I have never been intimate with anyone before." As soon as my words stumble out, she bursts out laughing, but not unkindly.

Pandora continues chatting away as she walks towards her closet and removes her spaghetti strap top, revealing a set of perfectly poised perky breasts. She then wiggles out of her high-waist jeans and glances in my direction, wearing nothing but a lacy G-string. My hormones race into overdrive. I drop my eyes and focus on the glass of juice in my hands, terrified that I might crush it to pieces from the pressure I am exerting on it. Desire for this magnificent creature overwhelms me.

Somehow, once again I manage to mumble, "Like I said, I have never been with a girl before."

I cringe as the words come out. She walks closer to me, sits down and removes the glass from my sweaty palms. I am tingling with excitement but completely confused about how to respond or where to look. The only other time I've been curious enough to Google 'lesbian intercourse' in the Comm lab left me extremely aroused, but doubting whether I would ever be able to pull off such intimacy.

Gently, she lifts my head and draws me closer to her. I can almost sense the pulsating rhythm beating between her legs. She seamlessly brings her lips to mine, gently locking us into an intimate exchange. My eyes close. I loosen the noose of anxiety that has kept me hostage and allow my organs to align to the tenors of the symphony of sweetness at play. When her hand moves down the nape of my neck I quiver with increased eagerness and let out a gentle sigh. She begins to unbutton my shirt. When I feel her hands move towards the mounds on my chest, I suddenly retract from the kiss. I tell her that I am not ready to move to that world just yet. The reality is that I am ashamed of the female form of my body. I have never been able to even look at my breasts or the *thing* down there – my body is a contradiction of my soul. I cannot bear the thought of another seeing the detested, inflated balloons that haunt my chest. She gently looks into my eyes and assures me that everything will be okay. I respond by politely removing her hands and proceeding to button my shirt.

In an awkward silence I grab my backpack as she pulls on a bathrobe.

"You really don't have to leave. Maybe we can sit and just talk or have supper and watch something on TV."

"No, thank you ... I have to go." Swiftly, I sling my backpack onto my shoulder and head for the front door without saying goodbye. I cannot imagine sharing parts of me that I am not ready to face myself. I hurriedly make my way up two flights of stairs to my flat without greeting a single person along the way.

In my bathroom I stare at my reflection for a long time. Although I feel confused, I know that I have met an amazingly beautiful young woman and have come extremely close to opening myself to the world of Pandora and the contents of her box.

☽

Back in the real world, the weight of my academic fees is weighing heavily on my grandparents. Uncle JS has taken it upon himself to assist me by sourcing funding. Despite my below-par performance thus far, potential funders are impressed with my matric results, but most are not convinced I have it in me to succeed at university.

I eventually get a breakthrough later in 2003 when a USAID donor agrees to grant me a full scholarship. Fully aware of the hardships I have had to deal with, they deem it fair that I be given one more chance to redeem myself. I no longer have to worry about empty grocery cupboards and all provisions are made to ensure I can focus fully on my studies. This makes all the difference. My marks and health steadily improve. It finally feels that things are on the up.

Towards the end of the year I receive a concerning call from

Ma telling me about correspondence The Mother has had with the university. By now, I have almost forgotten that I still have a biological mother, or father, and have tried to completely erase them from my life. The anxiety immediately returns. I can only imagine what vulgarities she has written in the letter. I try to probe Ma about the details but all she can tell me is that the funding office has handed a copy of the letter to my sponsor who has in turn passed a copy along to Uncle JS. Uncle JS has notified my grandfather of the existence of the document, which will be dissected at a family meeting at the end of the year.

I want the earth to open up and swallow me whole. I cannot understand why The Mother is trying to sabotage me again after staying silent for so long. I decide to speak to Birgit about it at our next session, and though I know she understands the traumas and anxieties that taint this nonexistent relationship with The mother, I hope the letter will be irrefutable evidence of the level of crazy we are dealing with.

But Birgit beats me to it. As I sit down for our session, she says, "The university has received some correspondence from your mother." I sit in silence as she continues.

"The contents of the letter are quite disturbing. I want you to know that this says nothing about you as a person, but speaks to issues that your mother harbours against herself."

Birgit scans my face for a reaction but I work hard to maintain my serenity. She waits for me to say something. Finally, I manage to speak.

"I don't think there's anything that can surprise me about this woman. After all she has put me through, it's safe to conclude that a person cannot put anything past her."

Much to my disappointment, Birgit does not reveal the contents of the letter. I insist that I'm not interested in what The Mother has to say, but in reality I really want to read the contents of this letter for myself. This woman seems determined to wage a new war against me, and I need to know what I am dealing with so I can prepare for battle.

When 2003 comes to an end, confident that I have passed, I

make my way back to Mthatha, the letter foremost on my mind. My grandparents welcome me home and make every effort at being extra sensitive to my needs. I feel like a loved child again, and though I have made a decision to stop taking my antidepressants and tackle my demons head on, they are lenient with my laziness and lack of energy for domestic tasks.

Finally my Uncle JS arrives and he too, like everyone else, is extra kind to me. We speak briefly about the year, my vision, possible goals – although all I really want to talk about is the letter. That highly anticipated discussion never materialises and, by the time he leaves, the contents of the letter remain a mystery to me. Mxmm. I am so annoyed. How can this large family of mine allow a single abuser to get away with such brutality time and time again? What is it about this woman that they fear so much that they would rather let a child continue to suffer indefinitely while seemingly stroking the abuser's ego? Whenever this woman wants to speak to any of them they jump at the opportunity to be in her 'good books'. I have reached a point that I've instructed them to stop telling me what she has said when she calls. I am simply not interested. But the truth is I am now obsessed with getting my hands on the now infamous UCT letter.

As luck would have it, my uncle has indeed provided my grandfather with a copy. One morning I walk into the dining room to find my grandfather engrossed in a pile of documents. I notice a letter written in bright red ink on top of the pile. I immediately recognise her handwriting. I scan it quickly, and manage to make out "To the Registrar UCT". I quickly back off. My grandfather never makes the mistake of leaving his documents lying around; they're always stashed in a secret place in his bedroom, where this letter is certainly also going to be kept.

So I slip into Sherlock Holmes mode. I monitor his routine for the following few days and am thrilled when one morning he announces that he has to attend a meeting with other former educators of the former Transkei, which will take place in the CBD. My redeemer must truly live, I smile to myself. The minute he's gone I inform my grandmother that I will be spring-cleaning their bedroom. She falls for my sudden interest in all things domestic. With cleaning equipment in hand, I do a quick scan of his closet – no papers there. Next I rifle through the documents stacked against the wall at the foot of his bedside table. Still nothing. I rummage beneath his bed, move their twin beds apart and even delve into my grandmother's side cabinet. This man has done a great job of hiding this letter.

Despondent, I decide to do some actual cleaning. As I pull the beds away from the wall, there, nestled between my grandfather's headboard and the wall, is a vintage russet leather briefcase. I crouch next to it, and open it. Lo and behold, third from the top of a pile of documents is what looks like the original letter The Mother has written to the university.

My eyes devour her red handwriting. I remain rooted to the spot. My heart racing, not certain how to quite get my head, my heart, my everything around what I have just read. I scan the letter a second and third time, and with each successive read I am more incredulous.

In a daze, I return the letter to the briefcase and carefully place it back in its original position. No longer in the mood to even pretend to clean, I leave their bedroom.

I lie on my bed, The Mother's malicious words spinning round and round my head. I spend the afternoon nestled in my favourite corner on the veranda overlooking the now rundown city that was once grand Umtata. There is a thickness in the air, a smog that creates a mirage of the city against the blue sky that is its backdrop. I know that I will have to address the contents of the letter with someone before my vacation comes to an end. My grandparents are out of the question as I feel a tinge of betrayal on their part. Since I've arrived home, they have continued to entertain their erratic daughter's bad-tempered calls. There is no one else I trust fully besides Ma. She will have to be the sacrificial lamb, the one who must suffer the rage of my discovery.

When Ma returns home later that afternoon I have worked myself into the foulest of moods. She tries making small talk, assessing how I am and whether I need anything. I have become a petulant child again. She pulls up a chair next to me. I take a deep breath.

"I found the infamous UCT letter and read it. I don't understand why no one showed it to me." I'm fuming.

Ma is shocked. "You know better than to go through my father's things. If he finds out, you and I are both going to be in a lot of trouble."

But I am in no mood for avoidance tactics. "This has nothing to do with you, Ma. This is all about me. I am no longer a child and since I am the subject of that letter it should have been shared with me. Why does everyone insist on overlooking me as though I am some fragile porcelain doll at risk of shattering into a thousand pieces?"

She has no comeback. My poor Ma has gracefully adjusted to my rebel self.

"I mean, what type of a person writes a letter to a university instructing the registrar to expel their child from the institution only because they have disowned that child? She even goes as far as telling them that I am not a Mabenge, the same bullshit she told me the day she called in 2001. She keeps alluding to this and I believe her, but how must the people I deal with regularly at the varsity – the people privy to this letter – look at me going forward?'

As my anger slowly subsides, the words I share with Ma come from a place of genuine hurt. Reading The Mother's hate-filled words, I have seen all the evidence I need that she hates me. "I thought by leaving PE, her life would be easier and she would somehow forget about me. Instead, she is determined to discredit me and ensure that I do not make it at university."

Ma tries to comfort me. "The best thing you can do is prove her wrong. We are not a family that deals head on with confrontation."

We sit in silence on the veranda. But Ma's words remain ingrained in my head: "The best thing you can do is prove her wrong." I have already wasted a tremendous amount of time and effort over the years trying to seek The Mother's affection and approval. It's time to fight back and excel.

The letter is never mentioned again.

TWENTY-TWO
Eye off the Ball

After having my best year yet, when 2004 arrives I decide to reward myself by fully exploring my attraction to women. I make it my mission to rid my wardrobe of any clothes that suggest feminine traits, save for the sports bras that are there to support my drooping breasts. Over time I begin binding them with bandages to give the illusion of a flat chest, an exercise that takes far too much time and induces much discomfort and pain.

My resolution manifests when I meet two delightful young women, Aziwe and Sizile, who will soon change the course of my nonexistent love life. I meet Aziwe at a house party at one of the resident's flats in Liesbeeck. She has sparkling eyes, gleaming white teeth and a smile that pierces the depths of my soul. I spend most of our initial encounter scanning her hourglass figure with curious eyes, allowing my pheromones to be unleashed. Although nothing physical happens between us, by the end of that night we have exchanged phone numbers and promise to keep in regular contact.

A few weeks later Aziwe introduces me to her friend, Sizile, who is much shorter in stature and lighter in completion. When she walks, Sizile exudes sexiness. She smiles a lot and strikes me as someone who is always up for a groove no matter what day of the week. We hit it off immediately and soon I am a regular at their flat, determined to always be seen with them because this makes me feel as though I've 'arrived'. We soon escalate to sleepovers and before I know it there are moments of intimate touching whenever the three of us are alone.

I'm in my element! These girls adore me and I am flattered by their rivalry around "who will bed Yolanda the most". I begin talking openly about these monkeyshine escapades, and before I know it I've earned a reputation as the butch lesbian from whom 'brothers' need to hide their women. I mean, come on! I am a psych patient, for Pete's sake!

Over time, I realise that Aziwe will make for a better companion. She is soft spoken and plays the role of the doting girlfriend perfectly. This includes cooking and cleaning for me and, on the rare occasion, washing and ironing my laundry. I find myself drawn to her compassion, and though I never expect anything of her, she always goes out of her way to make sure that all of my needs are met. Sizile, on the other hand, is foxy. She is a vocal feminist who has seen her mother subjected to the most appalling brutality, which is why she gives this lesbian thing a shot – at this point in her life, she can't stand men.

As far as studying goes, I have been far too consumed by chasing skirts, so it's little surprise that my mid-term exam results are below standard, despite having passed. Although I am upset, I'm not shocked when USAID bails on my sponsorship. I have spent most of the year focused on chasing beautiful women instead of diligently applying myself to my studies. So it is that I am faced with the reality of no funding; I can't seek further assistance from Uncle JS. This leaves me with no option but to play on my grandfather's emotions and ask him to stand as my legal guardian so I can apply for state assistance. The situation in which I find myself, however, gives me the wake-up call I need. By the time the year comes to an end, I have been approved for funding, although I will still have to contribute and I have shown a drastic improvement in my academics.

☽

The year 2005 sees me in my final year of my BCom degree. I have managed to get additional funding to supplement the shortfall. Mentally, I'm in a much better state and have firmly embraced my sexual orientation as a gay woman. I have long abandoned any efforts at ending my life and my therapy sessions with Birgit are flourishing. I have even managed to let go of much of my anger and vengeance towards The Parents.

Now I am eager to graduate so that I can start earning money. On the love front, I have casual relationships here and there, but always find time for my secret lovers Aziwe and Sizile. It truly feels as though the winds of change have finally colluded in my favour. Although I have been in regular contact with my family, I haven't been back to Mthatha for a while.

When Ma calls me on the morning of 6 June, I am over the moon to hear that she wants to gift me a substantial amount of money for having progressed to the final year of my studies. To the outside world I have been a time bomb waiting to explode, but to her I am her little champion who has stared adversity in the eye and, despite all obstacles, have emerged the victor. I remind her that I still have two sets of exams to complete before popping the champagne cork. I promise her that as soon as my career has taken off I will move her to Cape Town to enjoy a fresh start with me.

After the call I spend the afternoon in a truly happy place. I take myself shopping and use some of the money she has sent me to buy a beautiful corduroy charcoal men's blazer. Three days later Aunt PP calls me. It's early evening. I've spent the day with Sizile and we've decided to take our party of two to her place to close the evening off with a home-cooked dinner and a glass or two of bubbly.

"How are things going at school? Have you started writing exams?" Aunt PP asks. But before I even answer, she drops a bomb.

"I have some bad news for you." There's a long pause. My chest closes up. "Ma has passed away."

My heart all but stops. I fall to the floor, crumbling under the weight of the news. I throw my phone against the wall. How can it be? We spoke just a few days ago – we made a pact for a better future together. I storm through the flat, grief screaming from my bones. I thrash everything in sight. I pick up the wooden frame of a single bed and smash it against the wall repeatedly until it shatters in pieces. My anger rages. What sick game is this so-called loving God, who clearly detests me, playing with me?

I arrive home in Mthatha two days later, on the morning of Saturday 11 June 2005. As I disembark from the bus, I see Tando waiting to pick me up. The moment our eyes meet he tilts his head and welcomes me with a crooked smile. We share no words as he holds me in his arms before helping me with the little luggage I have. We are soon on our way home in my grandfather's vintage VW Passat. I break the silence with practical issues. It's too painful to speak about feelings.

"I will have to defer my last two exams for this semester. I spoke to my faculty – I need to fax the death certificate within five days.'

On the eve of Ma's funeral I am forced to confront one of my greatest fears head on. Earlier that day, my grandparents and Uncle JS had summoned me to a 'meeting'. They called me in to assure me that in the event of anyone from PE trying to provoke me or make me feel uncomfortable, I should walk away instead of engaging in any kind of hostility. There we go again ... I am furious. Instead of making sure that Stalin and her troops are cut to size, I am expected to submit. I huff out of the house, pausing only to request my brother to accompany me for a smoke as I fill him in on the meeting. As we stroll along the gravel road, puffing our lungs out, I inform him that there is no way The Mother will bully me this time. I am no longer a child and if she wants a fight I will gladly oblige and kick her ass to the curb.

The Parents and their two beloved children arrive later that evening. I want to throw up the minute I hear the car navigate the driveway. I am seated on the garden wall along with Tando and my half-siblings Nini and Mshumi as they approach the open kitchen door, just metres away from where we are seated. The gall The Mother has when she greets me is unbelievable, her voice laced with such falsity, as if nothing has ever happened between us. I watch as the rest of her family follow her inside. We have not seen each other since 2001. The thought of having them around at Ma's funeral, one of the darkest moments of my life, truly sickens me. I make a vow that night that I will never allow The Mother to see me in a compromised position again. She has done me a great favour by disowning me. I will use this to inspire me – as a launch pad from which to live my truth. My liberation will be her punishment.

○

After Ma's funeral I get back to UCT all fired up, ready to put everything into my final semester of studies. Seeing The Parents again has also prompted me to put everything into my sessions with Birgit. I need to find strategies to deal with all the messy anger that brews and boils inside me. The main goal in our sessions is that I clear the way for my studies to ensure that I show up with a degree when the time for graduation arrives at the end of the year. But there are more deaths in the family over the next few months, which see my grandmother having to bury three children and her husband, my beloved grandfather. I attend all the funerals and, as a result, most of my exams are deferred to the end of the year. I am now two modules short of graduation, with two supplementary exams to be written in January 2006.

I finally get my fifteen seconds of fame in June 2006. The euphoria I feel as I walk onto that stage and finally graduate is out of this world. It's been a really tough climb to get my degree. As the registrar caps me I realise I can achieve anything I put my mind to, whatever challenges come my way. I am alive and I have a beautiful future ahead of me.

I spend the rest of the year frantically job hunting. I go home on the odd occasion, but feel displaced most of the time because I now have no Ma or grandfather to talk to. On the other hand, my relationship with Miss K grows closer – she is the source of great encouragement and helps me with monthly expenses whenever she can. I finally get a breakthrough in October 2006 when I land my first job at the Woolworths Financial Services head office in Cape Town as an inbound call-centre consultant.

And yet, despite my successes, I am still plagued by the body I live in. I have been trying to shelve the nagging feelings that underlie my sense of belonging in this world. I try to speak to a number of psychologists about my predicament. I call LifeLine South Africa often. They are a free service and the anonymity of the space I experience during these calls allows me to unpack my frustrations around my body. I'm also encouraged to go online and read. I do countless searches for *being a man in a woman's body*.

I discover a wealth of information in the form of literature and online academic journals where my condition is referred to as 'Gender Identity Disorder'. Initially, I recoil from this label. I hate the word "disorder" as though there is something inherently wrong with me. Besides, my life has been chaotic enough up until now and I can't deal with a "disorder" that will hinder further progress.

So I resign myself to living my life as a butch lesbian, and am accepted as such by most people in my life. Then something significant happens in my search for identity – my friend Thandi re-enters my life in 2007. We rekindle our friendship. Although she has always known I like women, I have never discussed my suppressed manhood with her. I slowly open up and ask her to refer to me in male pronouns as "him" and "he". Without questioning, she obliges. Slowly I start asking other close friends to comply too.

TWENTY-THREE

Revisiting the Monster

When The Father contacts me one morning on my way to work at Discovery in 2008, where I had been employed since June 2007, I am completely thrown.

"Good morning, my child, how are you?"

My child? It is the first time he's ever called me that – never mind that he has no idea where I live, what I eat, or how much my personal life has evolved. I take a deep breath before responding.

"I am well, thank you. What's up?"

There is a long pause.

"I have some bad news. Your mother has been admitted to hospital and is currently in ICU."

I stay silent. When he realises that he has evoked no response from me, even though inside I'm a mess, he fills the space with specifics of her hospitalisation and the urgency of her current situation. She has apparently developed pulmonary edema and is in a critical condition. He is clearly expecting me to drop everything and board the first flight to PE to see her.

Hold up just a minute, Victor! So we don't talk for years – in fact, you and your wife disown me and try and sabotage my studies – and now you call me and expect me to respond like a concerned and loving child?

My actual response is measured and cold.

"I doubt this has anything to do with me. I am sure you are aware that this woman disowned me and threatened my education by asking UCT to expel me. So her being critically ill in ICU honestly has nothing to do with me. I have established a life for myself in Cape Town and am happy. I will not be making the trip."

I end the call. I hurtle my way to work through Milnerton in my little Beetle. I honestly feel no guilt or emotion at the thought of The Mother now critically ill. Minutes later one of The Father's brothers calls. He tries to convince me to see The Mother, but I make it quite clear that I am not going to pretend to play happy family now that their master is fighting for her life. But when the third call comes in from my brother Tando, my resolve to stay away is broken. He plays the guilt trip – and succeeds. I book a flight.

Later that week I land in PE and, within seconds of spotting The Father's face at Domestic Arrivals, I dissolve into a submissive panic. With years of living in terror under his roof, it is an instinctive response for me. I will later realise that these are symptoms of post-traumatic stress disorder. I talk myself out of the fear space and zoom into his eyes. They are dull and aged. I breathe easier with each step I take toward him.

Above my left eye I now have a brow piercing and am fully clad in a butch outfit with a double-breasted jacket. I've begun to grow my hair, which is now a full head of hazelnut-coloured dreadlocks. I have carefully chosen this look as my way of saying, "Don't mess with me. I am me, I am a rebel with a cause and I intend to leave my mark on all these people who have rejected and hurt me."

Thankfully, as agreed as a condition I will make this trip, Tando has accompanied The Father to the airport, so that I feel protected in event of an unexpected slap or fist in my face. As I approach them, my pace slows down. I manage a "hello". The Father reaches in for a hug and a kiss. I freeze. I offer a firm formal handshake instead, taking a big step back. I am in no mood for the pretence of happy family reunions. This is what I find most disconcerting about this man. At least with The Mother, she was always consistent with her cruelty and violent temper. The Father, on the other hand, could be loving and generous in company, but then, like a snake, turn into a man capable of the vilest atrocities. My brother's crooked jaw is testament to his violent cruelty.

The drive from the airport to the house is achingly uncomfortable. I sit quietly on the back seat of his magnificent Volvo and, with a heavy heart, feel a mounting dread as we near our destination. We pull into the driveway. The last time I was here was 2001, almost six years ago. Nothing seems to have changed. By the time we reach the front door, terror has set in and, for the life of me, I am unable to step inside the house.

The Father and my brother walk in, but my feet remained lodged in clay.

Although I know she is in hospital, I panic at the idea of The Mother emerging from her bedroom. Perhaps they have lured me here to murder me. "If any of my children ever turn gay, I will kill them ..." Her words wreak havoc in my head.

My alter ego urges me to turn and run down the hill towards Korsten, catch a taxi and head straight for the airport. Suddenly I feel my brother's hand on my arm, assuring me that everything is going to be okay.

"You sure that woman is not here?"

"I promise ... She's in ICU, at Greenacres."

Although I'm petrified that this is a set-up, I decide to trust Tando.

I lift one foot and place it in front of the other, and slowly make my way into the house to which I swore I would never return. Nothing has changed. I perch on the edge of the sofa. I'm taken aback that my childhood picture still adorns the wall. The Father sits down beside me. I want to run.

"We will be going to see your mother during the evening visiting hours."

I mutter an impassive "okay" and tuck my overnight backpack neatly into the space between my legs and the sofa. There is no way I can ever be comfortable here or risk demolishing the boundaries that so diligently protect my heart.

○

We arrive at Greenacres Hospital a few minutes after 7pm. I remain glued to my brother's side. My two younger siblings, Kaz and Ney, accompany us, along with The Father. We pile ourselves into the lift and make our way up to the ICU ward. I am not prepared for the army of relatives that awaits our arrival when the lift doors finally open. Standing in front of me is the bulk of The Father's family who reside in PE: siblings, nephews and nieces. I am overwhelmed. I haven't seen these people in years and here they stand, all eyes fixed on me, with broad fake smiles. I need to breathe and pull myself together. The hospital corridors are icy cold and I shudder at the idea that I will soon be forced to come face to face with her.

I tug at Tando's sleeve, and inform him I need some air. We move to the ICU entrance; I watch as different faces drift in and out. I could sit here the whole evening to avoid the inevitable. But my brother makes it clear that I need to face The Mother and that he will protect me.

As we approach her bedside, I stop. She is hooked up to machines programmed to pump life into her. Clad in a pure white hospital robe, she lies on stark white sheets and pillows. If I didn't know her better, one would be forgiven for mistaking her for an ailing angel. I inch a few steps closer, to stand my ground at the foot of her bed. On closer examination, the years have been unkind to her. I've read somewhere that we get the face we live.

The Mother is on her deathbed. Tando and Kaz urge me to move in closer. But I remain where I am. I'm not about to place my hand inside a snake hole and risk a sudden attack from someone I have learned to fear and distrust. I watch as my brothers caress her hands, talking to her as though she can hear them. I am amazed at Tando's ability to show compassion for a woman who, if her health were to drastically improve, would revert back to her old monstrous ways.

"I think you should come closer so that you can talk to her," Tando encourages me.

"I have nothing to say. I am fine where I am."

I truly do have nothing to say. The Mother has worked hard to destroy my life. Being in the same room as her is as much as I can give of myself right now. Then she looks at me, zooms right into me. I freeze in fear. I have one of two options: either stand there and challenge her in a stare down, or sheepishly tuck my tail between my legs and walk out.

I decide to stay. Our eyes lock for what feels like eternity. I try to read her thoughts, to sense what could be filtering through her mind as she continues delving deeper into mine. I gain courage as each second passes. When she finally caves in and shuts her eyes, I see a single tear trickle down her puffy cheeks. Within a second my hatred for her is reduced to pity. I have a moment of pure revelation: all that is required of me is to leave her to her truth and try to find it within my own heart to forgive her.

When she dies a few weeks later, I am back in Cape Town. On hearing the news I feel no sadness or pain at her passing, just a brief moment of disappointment at how she did not live to see my star rise.

I have been in regular contact with The Father over the past few weeks. When I disembark in PE for the funeral, he appeals to me to wear women's clothing as this is expected in their church.

"I have never been a member of this church," I tell him. He tries to insist. I suggest that he rather drive me back to the airport, insisting that I am not willing to compromise my comfort to appease the expectations of the church. In desperation, he ropes in his eldest sister, with whom I have a civil relationship. She repeats the plea The Father has made. I stand my ground.

"I am not willing to compromise who I am in order to fit in." Then I drop the bombshell. "I am looking into changing my gender so wearing a dress is something that is not going to happen."

My aunt tries to reason with me. "My child, you have to understand that everything you are going through is driven by the abysmal relationship you had with your mother. You are just rebelling psychologically against her."

Her reasoning is laughable. I watch her lips move. Her words fail to move me. It's clear to me that I am a stranger in this family. They have no idea who I am. I speak with quiet conviction.

"Like I said, I am not going to change who I am. If that offends you all, I am more than happy to return to Cape Town and you can bury her in peace."

I am on fire – my truth is blazing and no one is going to extinguish me. The Father caves in. I attend the funeral in my preferred attire. When The Father dies a year later from the same disease that took The Mother, no one tries to dictate what I wear to his funeral.

TWENTY-FOUR

Free to Be Me

The death of The Parents gives me new energy on my mission to investigate what it will take to finally embrace my journey into gender transition. I return to Google to locate organisations and institutions that can provide useful information. There is an urgency to my search. Since The Parents have died I have been moving between PE and Cape Town to help take care of the two younger siblings, through some sense of misplaced guilt, to try to help make The Mother's two youngest a functional unit again. But I feel like I am regressing. In PE I lose my self, while back in Cape Town I manage to live a life of freedom in my truth.

So it is that I find myself floating between two worlds. When I leave PE I always feel drained and deeply unhappy. Although I mask it well, I experience a deep hole inside and have even started convincing myself that I miss The Mother. I cling to a quote of the great American writer, Maya Angelou: "I've learned that regardless of your relationship with your parents, you'll miss them when they're gone from your life." The truth is that I am fooling myself into believing that there has ever been a relationship with The Parents. They were my torturers and abusers but somewhere along the line I find myself trying to change that narrative. This is often the case in the world of an adult trapped within a wounded child. It's only later that I understand that I keep returning to PE

142

to try to heal that damaged child in me.

Against this backdrop of tangled emotion, in November 2009, I begin hormone replacement therapy at the Groote Schuur Hospital Transgender Clinic. In all my quests to find answers, I have kept coming across an NGO known as The Triangle Project. The organisation solicits the services of a UCT sexologist, 'Ron', who sits on the panel of the transgender clinic, an institution I had never heard of until now. I arrange to meet with Ron at their offices in Observatory, and after a few weekly sessions, I am referred to the clinic for a thorough assessment that will determine whether I have a gender identity 'disorder' or not. Our sessions have inspired me to delve into the wealth of literature that opens my world to understanding the differences between 'gender' and 'sexuality'.

I arrive at reception at the Transgender Clinic and am greeted with great enthusiasm by the lone receptionist at the front desk. A few moments later I am ushered by a smiling Ron into a sunny room, facing the mountainside with streams of cars whizzing by on the busy M5 highway. After the formalities, I am briefed on what the journey of aligning my body to my true gender identity will entail. I will have to go through a number of assessments to meet the diagnostic requirements set out in the Harry Benjamin International Standards of Care for Gender Identity Disorder. At first I am deeply concerned at being branded with having a "disorder", but am reassured that this is only the vetting method, which can give me the green light to begin the long-awaited process.

For the assessment I appear before a panel of clinicians, including a psychiatrist, psychologist, social worker, endocrinologist, plastic surgeon and Ron, the sexologist. I am informed of the next steps, which will comprise three different sessions, the first with the psychiatrist, a few hours later with the psychologist and thereafter a brief physical exam by the plastic surgeon.

I am led out of the room by Dr Don Wilson, the psychiatrist, and can hardly contain my excitement at the opportunity to delve into my childhood with him. In his office I am offered a glass of water and a comfortable sofa. After a series of questions and reflections, Dr Wilson advises that I will be attended to by Dr

Adele Marais later that afternoon. I treat myself to lunch in the hospital cafeteria while familiarising myself with what I hope will become my second home.

When I walk into the office of Adele, the psychologist, later that day, she greets me with a warm smile. I am immediately drawn to her passion, as she explains why the standards speak to a disorder and how hormone-replacement therapy will impact my life if I opt to proceed with the biological alignment. We delve into a conversation similar to the one I have had with Dr Wilson. I am happy to share moments from my early childhood and the liberties my grandparents and Ma have afforded me.

After my session with Adele, I meet with the plastic surgeon Dr Kevin Adams, who leads me into a small examination room for an upper-body physical. He waits patiently as I remove my binding bandages and sports vest and requests me to sit on the examination table. When he is done probing my chest – he must have noticed how visibly uncomfortable I was – he offers his thoughts.

"Well, we can totally work with them. Your breasts are rather large, but don't worry, we can definitely give you a great chest."

"Geez, Doc – thanks a lot, hey!"

I have become accustomed to making light of conversations that involve my breasts. I hate them with a passion, I loathe the parts of my body that do not make sense to me. They compromise my identity, prevent me from being my true self. Conversations around breasts and mensies remind me of my otherness. A few years ago, on a particularly depressing morning, I even considered cutting them off with a giant breadknife. I had not yet done any research on why people are born in bodies not aligned to their gender identity, so thought it would be easier if I just took the matter into my own hands. My breasts stood in the way of me passing as a man. I truly felt that, with them gone, I would be able to embrace the displaced man in me.

With my history of mental illness, I knew too, though, that if I decided to act on my thoughts and take such drastic – and foolish – measures, I would surely face time in the loony bin, or jail, or both. What I knew for certain, though, was that I was

144

tired of not feeling able to get out of bed at times, of waking from traumatic dreams drenched in sweat and not wanting to associate with other people because it was easier to exist in a world where I was isolated. My breasts felt like the source of my shame and self-hatred. As I walked in from work that day, I slumped onto my futon-turned-couch and flipped through the TV channels, hoping to find something to distract me from the desperate thoughts plaguing me. Church-goers had told me time and again that it was not possible for God to make a mistake, that if He wanted me in a male body then that is how I would have been born. They neglected to acknowledge the other beautiful variations of gender, which included intersex as well as all the other non-binaries. My efforts at trying to convince them to think beyond their blinkered perceptions left me extremely drained and even more depressed.

That morning a few years ago I had decided I needed to do something. I walked to the kitchen and took a large breadknife from the utensil drawer. Out on my tiny balcony, I pulled out a smoke from my pack of Dunhill Lights, to which I had upgraded since I had started working, and began puffing, carefully considering the implications of slashing the unwanted breasts from my chest. I came to the conclusion that since no doctor would perform any procedure without it being a medical emergency, and since I could not afford any out-of-pocket procedures, I could take the risk, stomach the pain and hopefully incur so much damage that the doctors would have to perform an emergency mastectomy. But I was plagued by the thought: what if they could salvage these beasts? They would almost certainly commit me to a mental institution from which I would probably never be discharged. I finished my smoke and went back to sit on the sofa. I removed my chest concealers and noticed how my breasts sagged so uncomfortably on my chest. I stared at them for a while, the longest I had ever been able to look at my breasts in my entire life, and psyched myself up to prepare for the pain. With the gigantic knife in my right hand, I zoomed in on my left breast and, after much pondering, lifted it up and placed the edge of the razor beneath its fold. I took a deep breath and began moving my right hand in an up-and-down motion.

145

After a few attempts, I realised that I did not want to die, and if I lost too much blood – a distinct possibility – I would die here all alone. It truly was not worth the risk. I descended into a hollow of self-pity. Slowly, I lifted my behind off the couch and placed the knife back in the drawer.

Now here I am, three years later, taking a much healthier approach. I gather courage and enquire about the associated costs and what contraptions I can purchase to give the illusion of a flatter chest.

I am given a pretty straightforward answer by Kevin.

"Well, it depends on how much you earn. As a clinic, we can only perform four such surgeries per year and if you earn above a certain amount the hospital will charge you according to your earning capacity. It would be best to check with the Finance department for an accurate quote."

When it comes to breast flattening, Kevin cautions me against a chest-binding vest, due to the discomfort, but adds that a lot of trans men buy it from an international company called Underworks, which allows them "to 'pass' better with less dysphoria in public".

I decide to buy the vest. The bandages and sports bras are no longer working for me.

A few days later I am given the green light by the clinic to begin hormone-replacement therapy. My assessment feedback notes that I am "undoubtedly" a man who has had to find strategies to cope with living in a body not aligned to my core gender identity. As an affiliate of the UCT Medical School, I am informed that I will be exposed to a lot of students, particularly within the endocrine faculty. This does not bother me at all, as long as it means I will be able to start the process of fully aligning my body to my core self, which for me means alignment of the physical, though this is not a prerequisite for being transgender. I am requested to report to the outpatient department, where a folder will be opened for me and I will then be seen by the endocrine clinic.

I arrive super early on a Tuesday morning, and with the red tape of administration completed, I am asked to report to the clinic at 2pm. Until now I have been an extremely impatient person, but the dynamics of being a public outpatient quickly humbles me and I am taught all about waiting.

When the afternoon clinic converges, I am summoned into a room with Professor Ross and a few interns who talk me through the endocrine process: I will be weaned onto testosterone, starting with 50 milligrams administered intravenously every two weeks that will be increased gradually. They will also do regular blood work to ensure that my liver is not taking strain. The doctors make it clear that any form of hormone therapy subjected to excessive drinking and smoking with no physical exercise will hinder the process. In short, I have to embrace my journey with a sober mind and work with this new hormone to minimise any unnecessary risks. I am taken through a physical examination where the vitals are completed and recorded in my newly opened file. Then the doctors ask if I am comfortable with revealing my genitals as this will give them a better idea about my complete physical construct. They probably read the horror on my face and quickly assure me that I do not have to go through with this step if I don't feel comfortable. Despite the prying eyes, I realise that if I really want to work with myself, then I have to trust these specialists. I drop my boxers to the floor, all the while focusing on the scale at the far end of the room. After a few seconds of conferring, they thank me and indicate that I may get dressed. That wasn't so bad, I breathe with relief.

I am requested to hang around the consulting room a little longer as one of the doctors will soon return to administer my first injection. I chuckle to myself – my manhood depends on a vile of testosterone that will be carefully dosed out to me for the rest of my life.

The doctor returns with a vial of Sustanon and the equipment he needs to inject my behind. I smile. The waiting is finally over. I am now officially on this male bandwagon.

It is over quickly, and though I feel no immediate change, I know I have begun a journey of a thousand miles by taking this pivotal first step. I have entered the hospital a man trapped in a woman's body, and will leave a man emerging from a body that has trapped him all of his life.

TWENTY-FIVE

Trans-ition

I need to inform my employers about my journey, which will require me to visit the hospital every two weeks to receive hormone-replacement therapy that will continue for the rest of my life. To get permission for this I need to provide proof in the form of a letter from one of my doctors. But I am worried about the word "disorder" on the gender-identity confirmation letter. I fear it will create the wrong impression – that there's something wrong with me. I try to figure out how best to explain what transgender means and what my transition has in store for me and them. I've spent much of my own life confused, so how can I expect ordinary people to understand?

I begin searching the Internet for popular personalities whose journeys can serve as a point of reference. I also decide to delay any announcements to my family because I need time to adjust. Putting myself first, without pangs of guilt or obligation, is a first for me. I have got to the point of not giving a fuck what people may say or think of me.

Googling, I come across the name Chaz Bono and am immediately hooked by his transition journey. He is the transgender son of famous singing duo, Sonny and Cher, and there are facets of our journeys that are extremely similar. At some stage, he also identified as a butch lesbian, as I have. We are both chubby and he too started his transition journey to manhood in 2008, just like me. Chaz (formerly Chastity), though considerably older than me, becomes the poster boy I refer to whenever someone wants to know more, or whenever I am simply not in the mood to explain myself, which is almost all the time.

The first person I inform about my gender journey is Priscilla Coetzee, my immediate supervisor at work at Discovery. I have settled into my working life well and have grown as a person both intellectually and emotionally. But now that I will be receiving hormone therapy, I will be going through puberty again, until my body gets used to the changes. At the age of twenty-eight, there are bound to be emotional outbursts that might not be acceptable or understandable in a working environment. Ron has even offered to speak to my employer on my behalf, to explain the intricacies of how my transition will play itself out, and what support they can offer me during this time. I politely decline because I feel it's extremely important that I navigate this journey on my own. I'm pleasantly surprised by how supportive Priscilla is when we meet. She shows me great respect and voices her admiration for the courageous step I have taken. She advises me on how to approach my grandmother with my news and supports my decision not to consult the rest of the family until I am ready. Within a week she has up-skilled herself sufficiently and makes no mistake when referring to me as 'him', 'he' and 'his'.

I also receive unexpected love and acceptance from my childhood friend Lethu. She makes it brutally clear to me during a telephone conversation that she's in my corner.

"Chommie," she reassures me, "I've known you since we were in the eighth grade. I've seen you battle a lot of demons and skeletons in your life. I have noticed how you hid yourself and how you abandoned PE to find yourself. I would be going against the core of who I am if I were to deny the beauty I see in you. If the world turns against you, know that you will always have me in your corner."

I am left speechless. Given the centuries of social conditioning around gender transition, I tell her I expected resistance and even perhaps that she might disown me. Although I have known Lethu for years, I just never realised the depth of understanding.

Thandi proves to be a walk in the park.

"Mabenge, you do not have to explain yourself to anyone. If you are happy, I am happy, chommie."

It is around this time that I meet a group of guys working in various departments throughout Discovery: Mincili, Loyiso and Onkgopotse. These guys become my avenging angels. We soon start meeting on Friday evenings after work, which turn into extended nights out. We find strategic spaces to hang out, cognisant of the fact that I will always be the first one to break the seal and need a lot of bathroom interludes. Mincili takes it upon himself to design a roster for Fridays, which includes an hour gym session before we converge at our usual spot, Time Café, at Century City. We work hard and party hard, within reason for me of course. When the 2010 Soccer World Cup arrives in South Africa, we take an all-boys trip up to PE and literally vuvuzela the city to a standstill. It's amazing being in my hometown as me. The party continues back in Cape Town. What amazes me more than anything is the fact that, though the boys know I am transgender, not a single one ever misgenders or dead names me. They truly become the highlight of my life at a time that could have been extremely isolating.

I have also developed a few friendships in the trans male scene in Cape Town and, through the Triangle Project, have begun attending support groups, which prove very helpful. These are safe spaces where people who are gender diverse are able to share their journeys and the best practices regarding how to tackle the institutionalised politics that come with the various challenges of transition.

My new little world feels complete.

In February 2010 I even grace the pages of *Destiny* magazine. As a result of the spotlight that's been placed on Olympic athlete Caster Semenya, there's been a lot of media hype around the variances that exist in gender and sexuality. What concerns me most about all the scrutiny to which she is subjected is that no one seems too concerned about how she, the person beyond the label they ascribe to her, truly feels. I agree to go by my real name and have a photo shoot as part of the *Destiny* piece.

The one person I feel I owe a conversation before the article is published is my grandmother. The years have been kind to her, and she will be turning ninety the same month the issue hits the shelves. We have remained close throughout – part of my daily routine is a morning telephonic call with her. I spend many days and nights carefully preparing myself for the conversation and any possible rejection from her side. The day after the interview and photo shoot, I make a decision to shift our morning conversation to late afternoon, just before her midday snack. I line up her favourite arias on my iPod and plan to serenade her with Sibongile Khumalo's renditions of 'Della' and 'Isithandwa Sam' before delving into the business of the day. When I finally make the call, I listen on the phone earpiece while I hold an earphone to the mouthpiece. She hums, moving seamlessly between the different notes. When the songs are done, I tell her we need to speak about a serious matter. Nothing prepares me for the direction our conversation takes.

"So, Miss K, there is something I need to speak to you about."

"Okay, shlobo (friend), I am listening."

"There is a magazine called *Destiny* that I will be featured in this month. I would like you to ask someone to get you that copy so you can read about my story."

There is a brief silence and I assume that she might be thinking I have spoken about my terrible experiences in PE during the time with The Parents.

I build up courage and break the silence. "The article is about my transition journey. I am not sure if you are familiar with the term 'transgender' or not."

"I do not think I have ever heard of that term. What does it mean?"

It is now or never. I am not really scared, but I am worried. I cannot afford to lose my grandmother over something this important to me. I dive in.

"It means I was born in the wrong body. My body is one thing and my gender another. To put it clearly, I am a man who was born in a woman's body, and the only way to align my body to my gender is to undergo a physical transition. This means I will have surgeries to remove my breasts and ovaries and have a penis reconstructed for me."

What a mouthful. My grandmother and I have never spoken about relations and dating, let alone penises and gender. The anxiety hits me just as I finish my explanation. There is a long silence. Is she about to reject me? As brave as I have tried to be, the reality is that I cannot imagine a life without Miss K. If she has made a decision to reject me, it will destroy me. As much as I have been on my own for a long time now and can live without the rest of my family, this woman is my world, and the thought of losing her is unfathomable. Her silence is deafening.

"Miss K? Are you going to say anything?"

Finally her almost ninety-year-old voice speaks.

"What can I say? You have clearly given a lot of thought to this journey you are on. I do know that you have always been extremely boyish. I remember you insisting that you also be taught how to slaughter a sheep before you went to stay in PE. Your grandfather and I used to talk about you a lot. You have always defied every attempt at socialising you as a girl."

"Does this mean you are okay with this transition and will support me?"

"It is not for me to be okay. The only duty I have is to be supportive of you whatever you do with your life. When you were eight years old you told me you were a butterfly, and I told you to be the most beautiful butterfly you can be. The only fears I have about this transition are the surgeries. What if you do not make it out of the operations?"

I have not thought that far, but I do know this is a journey I have to take.

"If I die during surgery then that will have been the day my life was determined to end."

We leave the conversation at that and agree that if the surgeries make me happy then she will fully support me. I am awestruck by the love that this old woman has shown me. When I hang up and reflect on the beauty of what I have just shared with Miss K, I realise that there are truly amazing forces at work in my life. I have been raised in love, I have seen the brutalities of hate, and have returned to love. It is then that I realise that whatever happens during my journey, whoever I lose, whatever the outcomes of surgery, I will present as the truth at all times and that truth will be shielded by the few who see me and receive me for who I truly am.

Miss K and I never mention the specifics of my transition again, although she does enquire about my general health, and makes me promise to let my doctors know if anything feels amiss in my body. When she passes two years later at the age of 92, I bid her farewell with much peace in my heart. We have come full circle and no unfinished words remained unuttered between us.

○

I spend the rest of 2010 finding out more about the legalities of officially changing my given name from Yolanda to Landa and gender marker from Female to Male at Home Affairs. I am excited; this will give me greater control over my life and destiny. I often wonder how many children go through life drowning in misery over names they dislike but have to keep due to societal expectations. Screw society. I know that I would have changed my name at some point whether I was transgender or not.

I have never liked my given name, but I am also curious to find out who named me Yolanda and what that name meant to them. My research finds me back at Ma. Uncle JS is particularly helpful as he is able to tell me that after I was brought to Mthatha as a two-day-old infant, Ma took close on a week to name me.

"As I recall, I was at Rhodes in 1981 when you were born," Uncle JS tells me during a phone call, "but according to Nhomi [my Ma] she gave you the name Yolanda, inspired by the American Gospel singer of the time. The name actually means Violet. During that time there was also an animated movie with Yolanda as the Queen of the fairy land."

I'm not sure how I feel about being named after a gospel singer

153

or a fairy queen, but I figure I should cut Ma some slack as she never really planned on becoming a mother overnight. I am, however, touched by the meaning of the word, which, after much consideration, speaks to many characteristics I have grown to like about myself. So it is that I decide not to deviate too far from it. It has a lot to do with staying bonded to Ma, the woman who gave her life not only to raise me, but to love me selflessly with no obligation imposed on her by nature or biology. So I simply decide to remove the 'Yo' and gift myself 'Landa' as my official name. It also occurs to me that wherever my journey might lead me, and whatever ebbs and flows might follow, I can never erase the fact that I was born in a woman's body and that a part of me has been socialised and accepted as Yolanda.

When I walk into the Home Affairs office in central Cape Town later that year to officially start the process of changing my name, I have been known as Landa for over a year. There is a bitter-sweetness in my heart as I fill in the required documentation. The beauty about this process is that I do not need any reason to officially alter my first name. My application is two-fold: firstly, to fill in a BI-85 for the Alteration of Forename in terms of section 24 of the Births and Deaths Registration Act, 1992 and secondly, fill in a BI-9 First Application for an Identity Card. All I need is to put down my existing one followed by the new name and surname as it should appear on my new ID. I fill in both documents with an overwhelming sense of achievement and pride at having reached this point. The official attending to my case informs me that the process could take anything between two to four months as my name change will first have to be advertised in the *Government Gazette* for a specific period of time before my new ID document can be issued to me.

A few months later, in May 2011, I receive notification from the Department of Home Affairs, advising me that my new ID book is ready to be collected from the Home Affairs office in the CBD. When I open it and see my name Landa, the joy I feel usurps everything I have felt since I've begun my transition.

With my name officially changed, a year later, in September 2012,

I find the courage to send an email to every single member of my family with access to email, including the paternal side – against my better judgement. The contents describe my journey as a trans man. I allow them into my world, how I have gone about changing my name and how I am in the process of changing my gender marker. I describe what it means to be transgender, what the journey will entail and how I would appreciate their support going forward. Now that I have settled into stable testosterone doses and good vitals, I have reached a point where I am ready to rope everyone in, in the hope of support and love. I am also realistic enough to know, though, that those who harbour deep prejudice will choose to part ways with me – and I am okay with that.

TWENTY-SIX

The Bureaucracy of Gender

In early 2013 I prepare myself for war with the Department of Home Affairs. I've spoken to many trans people who've regaled me with horror stories of how, when trying to alter their gender markers, they've been met with ridicule and prejudice from officials, despite having all the required documentation. In all these cases, it appears that personnel have strong convictions on what they deem morally acceptable or not, and use the offices as an arena to deliberately humiliate transgender people.

By this stage, some of my physical characteristics have altered quite drastically. My voice has deepened, some body fat has shifted and I am passing well in public due in large part to the chest-binding vest. Although it takes a lot of effort to get it on, the results are worth it. I battle in and out of it every morning and evening, but it tucks in what needs to be hidden. Over weekends, I leave it on overnight as it feels great to have the entire bed to myself and not have to share it with the two unwanted guests on my chest.

In the meantime, I put all my effort into getting the necessary documentation to assist me with the gender-marker change application. The governing authority for this leg of my journey is the Alteration of Sex Description and Sex Status Act 49 of 2003. I need two letters to accompany my BI-526 application to be submitted to Home Affairs. The first letter is drafted by Dr Adele Marais confirming that I have for the last two years been living in the gender role corresponding to the sex description I wish to be registered under. The second letter is from my private GP, which corroborates that I am transgender. I decide to use the services of the Wynberg Home Affairs office in Cape Town.

This office is fairly new so I'm hoping the staff will be more open-minded. I arrive at the offices with a great degree of boldness and easily make it through the first hurdle and am allocated a ticket to a specific teller. The official is a young black gentleman. I look him straight in the eye and explain to him that I am submitting an application to correct my gender in the country's births and deaths register. He carefully scrutinises the contents of each letter. He then advises me that he has never dealt with such an application before. He excuses himself for a moment to confer with a senior colleague about what the procedure should be. I go into defensive, bring-this-shit-on mode and secretly place my phone on record to ensure that I capture everything that is about to go down. The gentleman returns and asks a host of questions about what it means to be transgender and why I am changing my gender marker. I try to hide my irritation and tell him that all the information is on the forms and briefly unpack the reality of "boy born in a girl's body and boy is trying to rectify that".

"Mr Landa, you cannot be impatient with me, sir. I am trying to help you and to do that I need to understand."

He has me at Mr Landa. The defence bubble quickly deflates. I am touched by this person's humility in trying to assist me. We work together to sort the application, placing the documents in an order we deem will work best for whoever receives it in Pretoria. After we are done, he informs me that the process will take between six and eight months before a decision is made by the Director-General on whether to approve my application. I thank the gentleman for his assistance and leave the office with none of the scars of transphobia I had anticipated.

With that box ticked, I zoom in on the money I will need to finance my surgeries. I chat with Dr Kevin Adams to seek his advice on which surgery to tackle first and the options available to me. The first option is to pay for the surgeries out of pocket as medical aids in South Africa regard gender-alignment procedures as cosmetic surgery and do not recognise them as a primary medical benefit but rather as being medically unnecessary for the survival and wellbeing of a person.

The second option is to get my name onto the transgender clinic's waiting list for surgery, but this could mean a waiting time of between twenty-one and twenty-seven years! As a full-time employee of one of the leading medical aids in South Africa, I find it ludicrous that health insurers deem such procedures medically unnecessary, despite the wealth of evidence and the expert views of specialists who work with transgender patients on a daily basis. I simply cannot afford to pay close to half a million rand for surgeries that could mean the difference between life and death. Most transgender persons, like me, who are gainfully employed, are forced to be part of a private medical aid as an employment condition. In my case, my employer has a cost-to-company remuneration structure with no subsidy for medical aid. This means that I pay full medical-aid premiums every month, but will never be able to access any transgender-related healthcare benefits. Furthermore, the laws of the country recognise and protect my rights as a human regardless of my gender and afford me the constitutional right to alter my gender marker – so why aren't the medical aids in line with my constitutional rights?

I decide to make it my mission to begin these hard conversations. Kevin and I start consulting various sources in literature to find ways around the stringent discriminatory laws imposed on transgender people by medical aids. We keep hitting dead ends. I eventually write to the Council for Medical Aid Schemes as a regulatory body and seek assistance in trying to challenge the discriminatory legislation. It does not make sense that insurers can employ discriminatory practices and deny patients surgical procedures they need. The council responds in a typical 'technically correct' manner to all my attempts and I find myself sinking deeper into the claws of frustration.

When we have exhausted all possibilities, we attempt to seek out the procedures to be paid ex-gratia. As a member of Discovery Health, I get hold of all the forms and request my doctors to send me motivational letters, with clinic evidence, so that we can motivate payment. In June 2013 I submit all the required data.

When I discover that they can't even get the terminology correct on their system between 'intersex' and 'transgender', I begin to have my doubts, and I start buckling under the pressure. I loathe waking up in the morning, and depression is slowly inching its way back into my life. I am irritable and, although I try to keep focused and positive, feel like I'm failing dismally. I've recently met Queenie and have fallen in love, but even pheromones can't keep the depression at bay. My old isolation patterns start to emerge again, and I find myself holing up deeper and deeper into myself. I drink – a lot – and find solace in my new friend Smirnoff 1818.

Even though the arrival of my ID document brings me happiness, I soon return to a dark place – none of this means anything if I can't find a way to get my surgeries done. I feel like the victim of a prejudiced system. The little faith I have in God evaporates as I drink and smoke my unhappiness away.

At the end of 2013 I decide to go home for the Christmas break but it's a nightmare. Without the love of my grandmother, I feel like an unwanted outsider and butt heads with anyone who dares to step on my toes. I wallow in self-pity and invest all my energies in hating myself. Again, my suicidal urges resurface.

TWENTY-SEVEN

Blackout

When I return to Cape Town in the new year of 2014, my downward spiral intensifies. Once really vigilant about getting my hormone injections from my doctors, I start administering them myself and, often too hungover to remember, weeks go by with me forgetting. My girlfriend Queenie is constantly on my case. It feels like she is the only positive thing in my life, but my mood swings are messing even that up.

While showering one morning I notice a lump in one of my breasts. A thought suddenly comes to mind. My medical aid offers one free mammogram screening a year. What if this lump turns out to be cancerous? I make my way to work and start furiously researching probabilities of breast cancer in males. Boom! Right there on Dr Google! I am now so desperate that the thought of cancer doesn't bother me at all; I just want a mastectomy, no matter how I get it. I secure an appointment at the Vincent Pallotti Hospital and count down the days in anticipation of the silver lining in what looks like a line of continued misfortune.

"They are not breasts, they're teabags."

I try to make light of my distended breasts as the mammographer requests me to take off the clinical gown.

"You know, the only reason I am having this mammogram is in the hope that this lump will be cancerous. That way, Discovery will have no option but to pay for a double mastectomy."

Her smile turns to a look of concern.

"Isn't that a bit extreme? Why would you wish cancer on yourself?"

I focus on her hands as she squishes the sanitiser knob and rubs her hands vigorously. She moves back towards me, her eyes fixed on the deflated balloons on my chest.

"Do you know why they look like teabags?" I ask and, without even giving her a chance to respond, continue: "Because I have been binding them from a very young age."

I watch as the blood drains from her rosy cheeks.

"Why would you do that, Landa?"

"I am a man ... a man stuck in a woman's body. So the reason I want it to be cancer is so that medical aid can pay for my gender-affirming procedures. At the moment, they refuse to do so. They've decided that being born this way is a choice, so the surgeries are regarded as cosmetic."

She doesn't respond. Instead she takes a step back, analyses my upper torso and asks me to move towards the machine. She gently places her right arm on my lower back and nudges me forward. She takes a few paces back to adjust the machine until my right teabag is perfectly nestled on the machine's receiving tray. She walks back to me and gently adjusts the teabag, ensuring it is perfectly centred.

"Okay, Landa, I'm going to begin with your right breast."

"Teabag!" I interject.

Paying no mind to what I have just said, she walks to her mini control station, eyes fixed on the screen in front of her.

"This is going to hurt a little and will be extremely uncomfortable. Please do not move. Stand perfectly still until I tell you I am done. Make sure to keep your head upright and look straight ahead."

Bitch ...

I dig my heels into the nest of my shoe and wait for the presser to make contact. The pain she has forewarned me of is a massive understatement. I feel my usually limp teabags amassing under the pressure of the presser. I retreat to my imaginary world, praying for a miracle. Perhaps if I beg her to press harder the contents will burst from the seams and the doctors will have to operate.

I imagine myself lying flat back in an ice-cold *Grey's Anatomy*-inspired theatre, chest slashed open to relieve me of the baggage I have been carrying for over a decade and a half. I return to the present when the presser lifts, relieving the pressure. The aftermath of pain is horrendous. She does the same to the other side. Same effect. I return to my cubicle to rebind my aching chest.

A few weeks later, the results of my mammogram come back. Negative.

I am plunged into a new level of reckless despair. The drinking and partying intensify. I constantly discuss my medical aid cul-de-sac with Queenie. One day we come up with an idea for me to join her medical-aid scheme as a spouse dependant and motivate to the new scheme for the payment of my surgeries. She is eager to assist as she has watched me spiral into a web of darkness. And so in February 2014 I officially withdraw from Discovery medical aid and join Queenie's Bankmed CareCross scheme as a spouse dependant. The beauty of the move is that the scheme has no waiting period, so I can start the motivation process almost immediately. But with this huge favour comes a great indebtedness towards my girlfriend. It feels like any hope for a new life depends on her, and our relationship comes under a lot of pressure.

Queenie has recently embarked on what she calls an "ancestral and spiritual awakening", a journey that will ultimately see her emerge as a sangoma. I manage to justify my drinking even more now, believing that the ancestors respond very favourably to Smirnoff 1818 and Viceroy gifts. In between the boozing I try to be the devoted boyfriend, accompanying her on trips to her ancestral school in Khayelitsha. It feels like it's the least I can do since she's agreed to load me as a spouse when she truly has no obligation to. That I'm paying my portion doesn't lessen the sense that I owe her.

Around the same time I forge a strong relationship with a female colleague at Discovery, a devout married Muslim woman: Nurahn Ryklief. When I confide in her about how uncomfortable I am about Queenie's ancestral work and the turmoil it's causing in our relationship, she warns me that things are not going to end well.

"Landa, you are trying to get your motivations and surgeries approved this year. I don't think you can be focused on both these journeys. I also don't believe you have any business being involved in that world."

I sense in my core that Nurahn is right, but I find myself torn. If I don't actively support Queenie, then I will look like a selfish bastard. I am under no illusion that I know much about ancestral spiritual work, but I do keep thinking that surely her blood family should be involved at some level. Queenie has, however, chosen not to tell any of her blood ties about her work so I am the one who is compelled to take part in the rituals whenever the presence of family members is called for. I find myself attending all-night sessions, watching the initiates dancing to the beat of a drum, trying to evoke the attention of their respective ancestors.

I begin to be drawn into this world, lost in hypnotic song and drum beats, and find myself wanting to know more. I start reading and researching the role of ancestry in the lives of black people; I am especially drawn to the idea of how the ancestors can bring good fortune and protection to the lives of the living.

This feeds my hunger to live the high life; I'm on a crazy wheel of spending: on alcohol and on Queenie, and my debts are building up. At home the arguments between Queenie and me intensify as I become more and more insistent that she involves her family. My gut tries to warn me to step back but instead of listening, I drown my concerns in alcohol.

By the time the Easter weekend arrives, I'm losing control. I've been warned not to mix the testosterone injections with booze, but I'm hell-bent on following my urges. So that I can get some breathing space, I encourage Queenie to go home to spend time with her people. At this stage I am feeling more and more like I need to get out of this dysfunctional relationship. On the morning of Good Friday, she drops a bombshell: she no longer wants to go. The day disintegrates into a mess of drinking and ugly arguments.

To ease the tension, we go to a jam session with friends. I drink a whole lot more. Later that night we make our way home together. Encouraged by her spiritual teacher, she usually has a nip of Smirnoff because "it helps with the clarity of the dreams she has while sleeping". The mood is civil and I accept a nightcap from a bottle she offers me. We retire to bed.

I don't remember what happens next.

When I finally come to my senses, I realise I'm holding one of my walking sticks. But why are the walls streaked with blood? Why am I stark naked? When did I get up? Why is the stick I'm holding drenched in blood? Oh my God, what have I done? *What have I done?* I hear a cry and my eyes start to focus until they finally settle on Queenie. She's circling the room in a daze, bleeding profusely from her head and other parts of her body. She begins screaming hysterically as I move towards her.

The screech of the house alarm sends a new shock of panic through me. I stumble to the bedroom and grab the nightgown I've inherited from my grandfather to conceal my bare body. The alarm wails louder. Now the sounds of sirens outside add to my rising terror. There's a loud banging on the front door, male voices. The response team has arrived. I refuse to open the door, but Queenie's grabbed the remote control to the garage. Before I know it I've been handcuffed and thrown in the back of a police van. My head's swimming, I'm trying to put the pieces together. I want to throw up.

TWENTY-EIGHT

Hidden Things

I'm booked in at the Tableview police station and tossed into a cell with other male inmates. I'm acutely aware of my nakedness beneath my grandfather's gown. I'm officially charged with assault with the intention to do grievous bodily harm. Am I fucking dreaming?

When the charge officer instructs me to walk through the events of what happened last night, I try to put the pieces together. I find myself telling him a long, complicated story about the life we've been living, the ancestral and sangoma sessions and about the literature I've been reading. I go into a lengthy explanation of evil and ill-intended sangomas.

When he asks me, "But what has happened to your girlfriend?" I am stuck for an answer. I want to tell him that I remember nothing, but instead I tell him that I believe she has inflicted the injuries on herself. I have even begun to believe this version of events myself. In the absence of a witness other than Queenie, there is no one who is able to dispute this. I cannot even begin to utter the words that it could have been me, gentle and kind Landa, who did this to her. I cannot face the idea that I may be responsible for her injuries. Instead, I convince myself she is the one who has brought evil into our home and inflicted the injuries on herself. The officer keeps writing. At the end of a long, long story, he instructs me to sign at the bottom of the page, thus sealing my fate. I am not sure whether he believes me. In fact, I'm not even sure that I do either. It's around 2am when I'm taken to a single cell, where I shut my eyes and search for sleep on a thin mattress under a bug-infested prison blanket.

On Saturday morning I'm granted permission to make a single call to my brother Tando, 1200 kilometres away in Mthatha. He promises me that he'll try to get me out of jail before the weekend comes to a close.

The day passes in a daze. How did I get here? *How the fuck did I get here?* When evening comes, I am shoved into another filthy cell with eight other men arrested for various crimes. By now Queenie has made a full statement of how I attacked her. I've managed to get hold of some clothes, including my chest binding vest – brought to the station by an estranged cousin Tando has contacted. It's some relief that I now have my armour.

The cell is cramped; it's exactly the same size as the single one I had been kept in, except it now houses nine of us. A few rays of sun manage to slip in through a small opening, casting some light on a line of thin mattresses covering the floor under a semi-sheltered roof. The central feature is an open toilet, and the stench of faeces and stale urine contaminates the air. I panic when I notice two scrawny gangster types with the number 26 tattooed on their arms. A few years ago I saw the theatre production, *Prison Codes*, at Artscape and am all too aware of how the number system works in South African prisons. The rest of the guys speak Xhosa.

Lunga, who's full of jokes and smiles, notices my discomfort and begins talking to me, asking me what I'm in for and whether I'm going to try for bail. The two 26ers keep looking at me from across the cell. I've placed my soiled mattress closest to the door in the vague hope that if I need to shout for help it's best that I am here. But more than any of the dark thoughts circling my mind, I'm terrified that someone will discover that under my clothing is a female's body.

I have been too nervous to inform the police authorities that I am transgender as I've heard brutal stories of transphobia in prisons where police officers have thrown a transgender man into a cell of men and told them to "enjoy" the female genitalia.

As night closes in, my terror grows. While the prowling 26-ers have retired to the corner closest to the latrine, I know I am easy meat. As though he's reading my mind, Lunga asks if I am comfortable where I am or whether I would rather move beneath the sheltered part of the cell. He helps me place my mattress in line with the other Xhosa inmates, and in Xhosa offers to keep an eye on the notorious two who he's also noticed eyeing me.

After supper, a nauseating mishmash of spaghetti and vetkoek, the lights are switched off and we retire for the night. For some strange reason, I feel safe. My gut tells me I will be okay, although I do still sleep with my back to the wall just in case my backside proves too tempting. I drift in and out of sleep, but every time I wake I see Lunga, sitting upright with his back against the wall, keeping watch.

I am relieved when I notice the first golden rays pierce through the bars. I have spent a night jam packed into a tiny jail cell with eight men who have no idea that I am transgender.

By evening a lawyer arrives with bail to secure my release. My brother has kept his word and come through for me.

The full reality of Good Friday night hits me when I get home to a blood-spattered apartment. It's empty. Queenie has left, and is staying with one of my estranged cousins. In a few days it will be my thirty-third birthday. How did everything unwind so quickly? A deathly depression descends on me. The red-streaked walls keep reminding me of what I've been accused of. I just can't find a way to believe that I could have beaten up another human being. I have flashes of The Father kicking my head, The Mother cheering him on, The Father beating and kicking Tando. After all the hatred I have carried in response to their brutality, have I inherited the curse of violence? Have I become my deepest nightmare? Am I now the carrier of the sins of The Father and Mother?

When it comes to the events of that night, I have a black hole in my brain. I need to speak to someone to try to work this all out, so I call Vo, an old friend I have not spoken to for some time, who happens to share a birthday with me. I tell her what's happened. She insists that I come over and stay the night.

The next morning, we go back to my house, joined by my cousin Minky, and start cleaning up the mess. In the spare bedroom we come across a Smirnoff nip bottle half filled with a reddish liquid, black beads floating on the surface. The outside of the bottle is caked in a greasy substance and nearby is a packet filled with what looks like dried herbs.

This all looks highly suspicious. I decide I need to find an independent traditional expert or sangoma who might be able to shed some light on our findings. The more I try to rationalise what has happened, the more I am convinced that there must be a sinister hand in the midst of it all.

After we've cleaned up the mess and wiped down the walls, Vo and I decide to find a mediator to try to resolve the matter between Queenie and me before it escalates to possible jail time. I am relieved when Vo says she's willing to sit in on the discussions. I can't afford a lawyer – my finances are in a terrible mess. News of the night spreads fast and mutual friends recoil from me; to them, I am the beast who beat up his girlfriend.

Vo and I decide that if anyone can get through to Queenie it's her sangoma, so we take a trip to Khayelitsha to speak to the woman, who I have got to know over the past few months. After listening to my story she pauses for a long while before offering her verdict. Her words chill me to the bone.

"Landa, I am not surprised by what you are telling me. I knew it was going to happen."

I have no words. I ask her if she can help mediate a conversation between Queenie and me.

"I do not have a problem talking to her and I know that she will listen to me. When all of this is resolved, both of you will have to make sure that you do everything I require of you, otherwise one or both of you will end up dead."

I am desperate; I feel like a beggar, prepared to do anything. Right now I feel I have no choice.

The sangoma calls Queenie and we all make the trip back to Parkland, accompanied by a group of elder sangomas she has organised. I am consumed by shame when I see the bruised and battered Queenie. How could I have done this to another human being? And yet, deep inside, I know that I have.

A long consultation ensues in which the intricacies of our relationship are laid bare and we are probed on our sexual life, which all but died almost a year ago. One of the sangomas points out that we are not siblings, and the reason we have got to a place of such violence is because we have been behaving like siblings and not connecting on a sexual level.

By the end of the session, Queenie agrees to drop the charges on condition that our relationship ends and I seek help for my anger issues. I end up agreeing to whatever is thrown at me.

It's decided that she and I will drive to the courthouse together on Tuesday morning for my initial appearance, after which she will inform the prosecutor that she is withdrawing the charges. I am deeply grateful for this resolution, although there is still a voice inside me that remains unconvinced that I acted alone in this terrible act of violence.

When Tuesday morning arrives, I pick Queenie up and drive to the court in the CBD. Outside my assigned courtroom we begin a casual conversation and even catch ourselves sharing a few jokes. Then she informs me that she's dreamed about us getting our relationship back on track, that she's even spoken to her mother, who has suggested that someone may have spiked my drink, which would explain the violence.

A few hours later we leave court with all the charges withdrawn and talk of rekindling our relationship. Her sangoma has suggested that Queenie moves in with her, and that I provide financial support until she is back on her feet. I, of course, am willing to do anything to make amends, but soon find myself deeper and deeper in debt. I end up driving 40 kilometres to and from Khayelitsha daily to support Queenie on the ancestral journey that she's resumed. I spend in excess of R3500 a week on petrol, drinks, food and other necessities she needs as part of this calling.

Other than Tando, my family has no clue as to what is going on, while my close friend Lethu tries as best she can to be a pillar of support from PE. I manage to show a brave face at work each day, I am filled with fear at the idea of anyone discovering what is going on in my real life.

Forced into Christian churches for most of my childhood, I have never believed in, nor wanted to explore, the different dynamics of my culture. Although Queenie and I have resolved our issues, I am plagued by a persistent urge to find out what the contents truly are of that Smirnoff nip bottle, now tucked safely away in a cupboard. I cannot make peace with what's happened, and I spend endless nights tossing and turning, wondering how I have got to where I am and whether there could have been more sinister elements at play. I read reams of literature searching for an answer.

Finally, I get hold of an elderly lady in the nearby settlement of Dunoon who agrees to come to my house and help me figure out what happened. A few weeks later I pick her up early one Saturday morning. As we enter the front door, she grows deathly quiet. She walks from room to room, and although it's a chilly winter's day, I notice tiny beads of sweat forming on her forehead. I bring out the nip bottle and herbs. Immediately she tells me to put them down. She opens the tiny bottle and carefully sniffs the contents; she looks upset. She shakes her head and, without another word, walks outside and paces up and down the back yard. Finally, she returns to the house and sits down beside me on the sofa. Slowly and deliberately, she begins to speak. She tells me that the house has a very heavy aura, one plagued by darkness. I listen entranced. She points to the tiny bottle and declares it evil muthi; Queenie, she says, must have been instructed to use it secretly. She then tells of things that have happened that make the hair on the back of my neck stand on end, things she can't possibly have known about. There is an urgency to her voice when she tells me I need to break things off with Queenie immediately because, though she is not herself malicious, she is carrying out the instructions of someone who is. She has been drawn in too deep and is in the process of dragging me down with her. I ask her why it is that I cannot remember what I did to Queenie on that fateful night. She then tells me something that pumps terror through my heart. She tells me that a "body number two" has engulfed me, and it has acted through me – that is why I have no memory. This, she adds, was exacerbated by the fact that I was drunk.

She explains that a shape shifter – one who assumes control over an unsuspecting person – took control of my body on the night. Yho! I do not know how to respond. I am more confused than ever. I have heard about the underworld and the dark forces at play there, but I am not sure whether I really believe it. Do these things even happen? My world, until now, has been limited to Western notions of religion and spirituality.

Despite my scepticism, a plan is made to invite my ancestors into my home through a traditional ceremony that involves brewing umqombothi, traditional beer, and inviting elders and friends to walk this journey with me. Although I have regularly travelled to my home in Mthatha over the years to conduct similar ceremonies – though more inclined towards the giving of thanks than an invitation for ancestral intervention – my knowledge is still pretty basic. I know that the ancestors are the spirits that float around us who are in the afterlife. These are the people who raised and loved us when they roamed the earth in human form. It makes sense to me that this role continues in the afterlife. Somehow, it feels right that I should try to reconnect with them.

The following two nights I immerse myself in prayer and meditation, trying to bring myself closer to myself. To keep my head clear, I drink less. I continue interacting with Queenie when I need to, without letting on what I have been told. In truth, however, I am struggling to keep the faith, battling to believe that I am an integral part of a life when deep inside I feel so dysfunctional, so doomed.

The ceremony inviting my ancestors' intervention takes place a week after first consulting with my new spirit guide. Before proceeding, I make sure to contact my family in Mthatha to inform them that I will be undertaking this untapped and unfamiliar journey. I am encouraged when Aunt PP and Uncle JS grant me their blessing. On the Saturday, a few elders I have managed to rope in through friends and my elderly spirit guide descend on my place. My cousin Minky is also present to walk this journey with me. The ceremony involves the consumption of umqombothi, and eating white samp and freshly slaughtered chicken. Then the men and women separate and continue indulging in the traditional brew intended to bring them closer to their ancestors.

After my traditional ceremony, I dream vividly. My grandmother appears often, always with a cautionary message. One dream especially stands out in which she warns me about the dangers of a world in which I am immersed. It's around the same time that I begin receiving calls from Queenie describing the "unscrupulous practices" she and the other initiates are being forced to take part in. She tells me that she's afraid to be in her sangoma's house as there are constant hissing sounds throughout the night. At times she is forced to share a bed with her sangoma, who keeps her awake with moans of pleasure, her legs spread wide apart as though she is engaged in a sexual act with an invisible man. I beg her to return home before something terrible happens to her. My greatest fear is that because her family has no idea about what's going on in her life, if anything were to happen to her I would not be able to give a proper account. I may even be blamed.

When Queenie does finally decide to leave, I arrive to find her packed and ready, but am horrified to learn that she has not discussed the matter with her sangoma. As a result, I am immediately seen as the instigator who is meddling in Queenie's journey. We leave amid a chaotic exchange of words and curses directed at both Queenie and me. We are warned never to set foot in the sangoma's dilapidated shack again.

That night, for the first time in months, Queenie and I truly connect and delve into the dangers of having embarked on a journey she has effectively been clueless about. I decide to be upfront with her and establish boundaries: I need to focus on my transition, and secure funds for my surgeries. I can't be messing around in a world of darkness I do not understand or belong in. Queenie does a complete turnaround and, in fact, thanks me for saving her life, leaving me more confused than ever, given the traumatic events of the past couple of weeks.

We try as best we can to rekindle the relationship, and focus our energy on getting scheme approval for my surgeries.

TWENTY-NINE

The Beauty of Flat

I research a number of plastic surgeons funded by the scheme in the event that my procedures are approved, but decide to return to Kevin Adams whom I consulted back in 2009.

He promises to personally present my case to the decision makers at scheme level in the event that they need further justification as to why the procedures I am seeking are indeed a medical necessity. I am amazed by Kevin's commitment and passion. He spends endless hours on the phone with me and responds to emails no matter what time I send them.

We resubmit the initial motivation, which includes the letters from the endocrinologist, plastic surgeons, psychiatrists and psychologists. Our goal is to ensure an air-tight application that covers every possible rebuttal the scheme might throw at us. To strengthen the application further, I track down Birgit Schreiber, who has by now assumed a senior position at the University of the Western Cape, and request that she assists with a letter of motivation. I make the trip to her offices on a Wednesday afternoon and, within seconds of seeing each other, we fall into an embrace. She commits her unwavering support.

So it is that, at the end of May 2014, I submit my full motivation to the scheme and begin the long wait. A few weeks later I receive a response advising that my request has been declined as "gender-reassignment surgery is a scheme exclusion". I am gutted. That evening I speak to Queenie, who encourages me to give it another shot. Before doing so, in desperation, I contact the scheme administrator telephonically and inform her that I will be submitting the motivation again and that my plastic surgeon, Kevin Adams, is willing to make presentations on why these surgeries are crucial to my wellbeing. It is as though a light bulb suddenly switches on – she knows Kevin! She tells me she will contact him directly with further questions. Finally, a tiny streak of hope breaks through the dark clouds. The phone call begins a series of events that spark a vested interest in my case by the scheme's medical advisor. I am requested to consult with a gynaecologist, who will provide further insights into the procedures I will need to remove my ovaries, preferably in a non-invasive manner. I do as instructed and submit all the required documents, hoping with each click of the Send button, that I am getting closer to the goal post.

A month later, on a cold morning in June 2014, the waiting comes to an end when I open my email: *Dear Landa, the scheme has approved your ex-gratia application for surgical intervention based on gender alignment.*

I can hardly contain my excitement. I leap from my desk at work and run over to Priscilla's office to inform her of the good news. She has been my most trusted supporter at work since the start of my five-year journey.

"I am so happy for you! I knew you were going to get this done. The moment I first laid my eyes on you in your red velvet blazer I knew there was something particularly special about you."

We are both close to tears. I make a call to Queenie, who too erupts in elation. We have been trying to rekindle our relationship, but the violence that erupted over Easter continues to lurk in the background, and the good news is a much-needed glimmer of hope that helps us to shelve all the bad memories, even if it's just momentarily.

I experience my first real joy in months when I forward the letter to all my doctors, with an urgent plea for the first available surgery date for the removal of my tedious teabags and ovaries.

Four months later, in late October 2014, I'm booked into the UCT Private Academic Hospital for a double mastectomy. Kevin is to be my plastic surgeon. We have walked a long, long road together, and I am ecstatic. I tell anyone and everyone who cares to listen about my transition and what a breakthrough it is for me. Queenie has taken leave to accompany me to hospital. She just about crawls under the bed in embarrassment when I walk around the half-filled, eight-bed male ward, introducing myself to all the gentlemen I will have the pleasure of sharing the space with over the next few nights. When Kevin arrives later that afternoon I feel like a delirious dog with two tails. I am excited beyond belief about where I am headed.

"You ready, Landa?"

"As ready as I will ever be, doc."

"We should be good to go within the next half-hour."

When the theatre crew picks me up and wheels me to theatre, I am in a jovial mood and chat up a storm, telling anyone who will listen that this is a moment that will go down in history: I am the first known transgender man in South Africa who has successfully got a medical aid to fund gender-realignment procedures through the Transgender Clinic. I can't stop talking about how this procedure is a big "fuck you" to all the other medical aids that have been giving me so much grief about paying for my surgeries. Before I'm wheeled in, Queenie snaps a couple of pics in the hallway. Suddenly the bladder that I emptied just a few minutes ago needs to take another leak. As I sit on the icy toilet seat, peeing my anxiety away, I whisper a small prayer of gratitude, asking my ancestors and the universe to walk with me.

◯

I wake up from what seems like a five-minute power nap and, half in a daze, instinctively raise my hands towards my chest to feel if they are still there. They're gone. It's flat! A recovery nurse approaches with a beaming smile and asks me how I feel. I look deep into her eyes. "They're gone."

"Yes, they are Mr Mabenge. Your procedure was a resounding success and we will be taking you back to the ward now."

I return to the ward to find Queenie waiting for me. She's been fielding calls from my family the entire day. None of them has been able to make the journey to offer their support in person. Unsurprisingly, not a single paternal family member has called.

Kevin walks in with a grin on his face and examines my vitals, congratulating me on a successful surgery. He informs me that my left breast had given him a little trouble, which resulted in an increase in theatre time from the projected two hours to just shy of six hours. But, overall, it's been a great success and, depending on my condition the following day, I should be cleared to go home within the next forty-eight hours.

I walk out of the hospital two days later a new man. I hardly feel any post-surgery pain. Instead, I carry the drainage containers attached to tubes still embedded beneath my skin with great pride. It does not bother me that I will be confined to bed rest for a few days, or that I will feel a measure of discomfort over the coming months. What matters is the beauty of the work on my now flat chest and the elation I feel now that I am one step closer to being absolutely free to be me without the physical burdens that have weighed me down for so long.

○

Two weeks later, flat-chested and smiling, I stroll into the UCT Private Academic Hospital for my second procedure and make my way to the reception area where I fill out the paper work. The friendly receptionist makes a call to the male ward to confirm my bed number. She suddenly looks concerned and tells me she needs to double check the actual procedure with the relevant doctor, as there seems to be a mistake on the system. Mistake? She informs me that I have been assigned a gynaecological procedure, but clearly that's impossible because I'm a male. I laugh, and reassure her that there is no error – that this is indeed the procedure I am booked in for. She repeats herself.

"I'm sorry, Mr Mabenge, but it is impossible that you're here for a laparoscopic hysterectomy."

I clench my teeth, trying not to laugh. "My dear, I am here for that procedure. I am booked under Dr Femi Olarogun."

"Yes, I see that, Mr Mabenge, but a man can't have a hysterectomy – it's biologically impossible. I'll have to call the sister in charge of the male ward to check with her."

I get impish enjoyment at her confusion as she makes the call. "Mr Mabenge, please speak to the sister."

I confidently take the phone.

"Mr Mabenge, I believe you're here for a gynaecological procedure, sir. I am afraid it's simply impossible for a man to have a hysterectomy. Are you certain that that is what you are here for?"

I pause for a moment, realising that I am about to push this poor nurse into cardiac failure.

"Sister, I'm transitioning from what is known as female to male. That's why I am a man who needs to have a hysterectomy."

Embarrassed and flustered, she thanks me and voices her eagerness at having me in the ward within the next few minutes.

In no time my documents are processed and I'm escorted to the male ward section, where I'm shown to my bed. I place my overnight bag inside the allotted locker and remove my clothes. The scars are still fresh from the double mastectomy and I briefly marvel at my flat upper torso in the half-length mirror on the wall closest to the small bathroom.

I breathe deeply, taking it all in. It's taken thirty-three years to get to this point. This time, though, I am on my own. Queenie has not taken leave; the relationship has been under a lot more strain recently. Soon after I settle in, I am greeted by the surgeon, Femi, who gallantly waltzes in and assures me that the less-invasive procedure will ensure minimum healing time. The level of professionalism he shows is remarkable. Although he admits he's never dealt with a transgender person before, he makes no errors in the pronouns he uses when addressing me. He puts me at ease in the way he sees me and receives me. I spend the rest of the morning in bed, allowing myself to be probed by the nurses to ensure all vitals are in order. The procedure is only booked for later that afternoon. There's plenty of time for me to reflect on the magnitude of the events of the past few weeks.

I cannot remember the last time I've been so happy.

When I'm finally wheeled into theatre for my second procedure, by mostly the same crew as a fortnight previously, I feel like a real regular. The laparoscopic procedure, which is completely non-invasive and will leave no visible scars, goes according to plan.

I wake up a few hours later and, unlike my double mastectomy, which is still in the process of healing, there are no outward signs of my operation. I am assured that everything has gone well and that I will soon be on my way home for the next leg of my recovery. I had already stopped menstruating five years ago, within a month or two of starting to take testosterone. Now I am absolutely guaranteed that I will never bleed again. Later that night I feel extremely vulnerable when the nurses on duty have to change my sanitary swabs and bathe me down there as I am yet to have my genital surgery. They, however, correctly refer to me as Mr Mabenge and treat me with such care and respect that I decide to fully place my trust in them, and though I know that they might not fully grasp what I am going through, they choose to see and receive me as the man I truly am and afford me that dignity.

Queenie picks me up the following morning. When I get home I am ecstatic. I am invincible. At the follow-up appointment a week later I am given the all-clear and I am all set to take on life and truly fly as Landa. My body has been through two life-changing surgeries in two weeks. I recover seamlessly, and within three weeks I'm back at work. The world is my oyster. But I will soon discover, like Icarus, that flying too close to the sun can be dangerous.

THIRTY

When Love Turns to Ash

With my new sense of self, I am unstoppable. If my body can endure all that it has, I can rule the world and celebrate in whatever way I choose to. Omnipotent, with unlimited power – god-like even – is how I feel. I throw myself full tilt into party mode, drinking up a storm, telling myself that this is all about toasting my new lease on life. I start moving in circles I know are not good for me, people who spend copious amounts living the high life, partying and consuming crates of ridiculously expensive alcohol.

And now that my surgeries are done I begin to obsess about the direction my love life has taken. Although I am truly grateful for Queenie's help in getting me on her medical aid and walking this important leg with me, I have become increasingly uncomfortable in our relationship. I still feel she has a lot of explaining to do about her ancestral journey, the one that so deeply affected our relationship, and whether she is still vested in becoming a sangoma. What I do know is that I am no longer in love with her, but because of the help with the medical aid, I feel obligated to stay with her. I am all too aware that, as much as I am celebrating my new freedom, at home I am not living my truth.

So, as I try to escape the real problems between us, we party relentlessly. Most weekends we return home in the early hours of the morning and try not to engage in any dialogue until we are both sober. We have agreed on this strategy to ensure that no violent episodes ever erupt between us again. Whenever I feel even a hint of irritation or dissatisfaction with her I have to keep some distance between us, my hands behind my back. Sometimes she demands that I stand in the back yard with the sliding door between us so that she can be assured that I won't attack her. It disturbs me deeply that we have got to this level in our relationship. Is this what love is supposed to look like? I feel like her stooge, like she has this power to remotely control my every move, thought and feeling.

In reality, all we are doing is living a hungover and meaningless existence, and towards the end of 2014 things have reached rock bottom between us. Queenie has become increasingly withdrawn and secretive. Some nights she doesn't come home at all. When I find a number of love letters from unknown men, it's clear to me that she is moving on and only staying with me for convenience. Because she doesn't contribute towards the running of the home, my financial woes are worsening and, fuelled by anger, I find myself having obsessive conversations with myself. As much as I claim I no longer care about the relationship, I feel highly disrespected – we are, after all, still a couple, however messed up the dynamics.

The more Queenie withdraws, the more I get lost in my trusted old friend Smirnoff 1818 to numb all emotion. I move through my days in a zombie state. My work begins to suffer. At my wits' end, I make an appointment with Independent Counselling and Advisory Services through my employer to assist me with counselling sessions; I'm desperate to get my life back on track.

One Saturday afternoon in December 2014, Queenie returns home from working 'overtime' and discovers me drinking heavily with acquaintances who live a few houses away. We leave for home and as soon as we enter the house she tells me I am consuming way too much alcohol, that she's not willing to risk "endangering her life again". We are once again entangled in an argument about the state of our relationship. The alcohol makes me loose tongued and I accuse her of having affairs and cheating. Without a word, she walks out of the house, slamming the door behind her. When I run after her, trying to convince her to return, she retaliates by telling me that she's never loved me and she is no longer interested in being with me. I am deeply hurt by her outburst and, without another word, I allow her to walk away.

But her cruelty has triggered something extremely painful within me, something excruciating. I sense that I am on the verge of losing it. I lock myself in the house, drenched in my hatred for her. The more I sober up, the more I pace up and down the house, convincing myself that this girl is nothing but a gold digger who has used me for the past two years, placing my life in danger by introducing the dark and dangerous forces of the underworld into my life, a world I never knew existed before I met her. I am torn up inside, triggered further by the years of cruelty from my childhood. I keep seeing flashes of The Mother's hateful smirk. Self-hatred consumes me. What a fool I've been to believe that I could be loved. I keep replaying events of the past year with Queenie and this serves only to escalate my anger and disgust.

I find myself in the second bedroom that houses all Queenie's clothes. I stare at the bulging cupboard and realise that when I met her she came into the relationship with very little – the big chunk of what she owns has been purchased by me. Her cruel words – how she's never loved me – keep echoing in my head. In a swift move, blinded by rage, I scoop her clothes from the shelves and carry the huge pile towards the open sliding door leading out onto the back yard. There's a built-in braai that has hardly been used since we moved in.

I watch as her clothes burn in a blaze of orange against the backdrop of the black night. It feels so right; this is the way I am able to even the score between us. The fire crackles, emitting luminous neon-coloured flames. I survey the raging furnace of fabric and, for a moment, I lift my head towards the heavens, thanking The Mother for my predetermined fate. I have proved her right: I am wholly unlovable, but I will go down with my head held high. It is not long, however, before my rage-induced courage descends into self-pity and anguish, as Queenie's wardrobe is reduced to ash, just like our relationship – nothing but grey dust.

I am immediately consumed by overwhelming regret.

Queenie arrives the next morning with a convoy to fetch her belongings. She has not seen her empty cupboards, nor the mess of black melted plastic mixed with ash outside. She brazenly announces that she wants nothing more to do with me and that her "duty" towards me is over. I later hear that all she's ever felt is pity for the "poor boy stuck in a woman's body" and has only stayed because she felt sorry for me. When I inform her that I have burned all her clothes, she turns to her chief female negotiator and, with a smirk that eerily resembles The Mother's, announces: "I told you 'he' – or whatever 'it' is – is a nutcase." And with that said, they leave.

Her parting words cut me to the bone. I wallow in self-pity. I feel the ache of my aloneness. I touch the scar on my left wrist. It is throbbing, calling me back to suicidal waters. Deeply depressed, I call Lethu in PE and inform her of what I have done.

"Mabenge, I think you have reached a very low point in your life. You need to take time out to seek help. There is a void that you constantly seem to be trying to fill with women who are drawn to you through pity instead of your beauty."

News travels fast in Cape Town. Later that day, I receive a call from my long-lost friend Thandi, who has got wind of what's happened. She begs me to go see her. When I arrive she's frantic, in a state of panic.

"Chommie, what happened?"

I sit on her burgundy sofa and relay the events of the past two years, giving her a blow-by-blow account of the relationship in which I had become entangled. I tell her I have no way out and am sure that Queenie will succeed in having me arrested for destroying her belongings. Thandi doesn't hold back and I am in no state to argue.

"Mabenge, over the years I have tried to steer you away from this mentality of tying yourself to women based on their physical beauty. You thrive on jumping into relationships with people you have not spent time getting to know and, as your friends, we are the ones left to pick up the pieces. I wish you had asked me about Queenie before committing to her since I was the one who introduced you to her in the first place. I would never have allowed you to get into this relationship, especially given your extreme personalities."

I absorb every word Thandi throws my way, knowing that she has my best interests at heart. She notices how defeated I appear and gently turns the focus of her chastisement to one of encouragement.

"Chommie, you need to realise that you have a unique soul, with an important purpose on this earth. You cannot go through life plugging yourself into sockets that are not for you to plug into. You need to bring your focus back to you and rediscover the vision you once had for your life."

As I sit listening, I realise how much I have betrayed everything I once believed in, including myself.

"Look, we are where we are now. We'll take Queenie as she comes and figure it out as we go along. In the meantime, it'll serve you best to speak to your Uncle JS and inform him of what's happened."

Fuck it. How am I going to tell my uncle that I have failed so dismally? But I agree with Thandi; he needs to know, and the only person to tell him is me. Shaking inside, I make the call. His response floors me.

"What do you think she is going to wear now?"

Ouch. I knew he would be firm, but I had not expected this. He is seething. Of course I should have thought this through before acting out on my anger. I have no words. Uncle JS slams the phone down and I know the shit has hit the fan. A few minutes later he calls back with instructions that I need to attend anger management sessions and refrain from any intimate relationship until I have completed the course.

When Uncle JS speaks, you listen.

So it is that I spend the remainder of December religiously attending sessions with an independent psychologist, with a focus on anger management and forgiveness. Uncle JS, Lethu and Thandi are my pillars during this time. I have moved out of the house of misery onto Thandi's couch and become like a little child to whom she tends with a great deal of love and compassion. Uncle JS calls me daily and brings me up to speed on how to deal with the pressures and anger that come with taking testosterone. He becomes like the father I have longed for and helps me by unpacking aspects of my childhood I have never dealt with, encouraging my healing through daily SMSes. I confide in him about the negative words The Mother drummed into me throughout my childhood, particularly those that entrenched the belief that I am destined for failure in my life.

"Mtshana, your mother was a very angry person. She made a point of breaking you down with her words. You need to realise that your destiny lies with you, and not with what others thinks or say about you. I trust that you have now learned that the only shame is having shame when you know you need help."

THIRTY-ONE

Operation Landa

I slowly emerge from my shell of isolation and begin clearing my life of all the toxic clutter I have collected since childhood. I remember the teachings of my grandmother – in particular, the advice to "shy away from idle company" as this is "the devil's workshop". The truth is that all the time I've been seeking acceptance and the good life, all the friends and lovers I have accumulated have brought me nothing but trouble and strife. I have been so caught up with my transition, aligning my outward self to my core by way of surgery, celebrating by partying and drinking, that I have forgotten to pay attention to the healing of my inner wounded child. All this denial and avoidance have almost derailed me. So many of my thoughts about myself remain clutched in the claws of The Mother.

I rent a cosy apartment where I can continue focusing on my emotional health and healing. I know I have to find closure around my childhood and a way to forgive The Parents, who I have spent much of my life despising, even in their death.

I have removed myself from Queenie and her circle despite the body shaming and name calling messages she sends whenever she feels like it. I am still being bombarded by messages. It's almost as though she finds pleasure in picking me apart. I struggle to find a way to stand back and not take her cruelty to heart, but I do. I realise that she is coming from a place of hurt, some of it caused by me, so she feels justified in lashing out at me. It's not always easy for me to take the higher ground because her words still traumatise me and, at some point, I hit back as hard as I get. It takes an intervention from Thandi and Lethu for me to finally block all contact with her and her crew, so that I can continue to piece together the fragments of my life. This inner work demands great strength and there are times that I fear that the pain will consume me.

I find solace in books and choose to read works that will help me find the way back to myself. I stumble across *The Art of Happiness* by the Dalai Lama, a book I bought years ago. I am particularly captured by this line: "Right now, at this very moment, we have a mind, which is all the basic equipment we need to achieve complete happiness." It reaches me deep into my soul. That, in essence, is what I have been missing my whole life – complete happiness. And it is my mind, my responsibility to create it.

I decide once again to turn to Uncle JS and begin weekly telephone conversations during which he encourages me to put the fragmented pieces of myself together, bit by bit. In between he regularly sends me emails with documentaries and motivational videos to bolster my fragile self-confidence. We work on strategies to curb the onslaught of resentment and come up with ways to ensure that I have no idle moments that will thrust me back into the dark hole I am working so relentlessly to crawl out of. Lately, I have developed an almost burning obsession with wanting to clear my name and finding plausible reasons to explain what happened on that fateful night when I attacked Queenie. The over-thinker in me is challenging me to find out more about the darkness of the spirit world, but Uncle JS guides me with his sage wisdom, encouraging me to make only positivity choices.

"The spectrum of life is comprised of elements of good and evil. A person needs to choose which to invest in. I can never discount what you have gone through or tell you it is a figment of your imagination. There are certain things we cannot quantify in human terms as they occur in the spirit realm, which, too, is made of good and evil. I trust you will henceforth choose good, as nothing worth investing in ever came from evil."

Thandi echoes his sentiments.

"Mabenge, you know I don't believe in that life. I am not saying it does not exist, chommie, but you know better than to invest in a world that is not yours to exist in. Stop being your own worst enemy."

And the more I read, the more I realise that I have become complacent in a life that has sucked me dry and diminished the ambitions I once had. Other than Uncle JS, I have no mentors, no immediate goals and no strategies to live a fulfilling existence. When reflecting on the years between university and where I find myself in 2015, I realise that my only real achievement has been getting the medical aid to pay for my surgeries, but that's old news. There is nothing I have stood for, no cause I have made a difference towards – frankly, I've partied and Smirnoffed the last few years away.

But, try as hard as I might, I remain rooted in the shame of having lost out on love, which seems to have become a cruel pattern in my life. I have long conversations with Uncle JS in which we try to unpack the reasons for my shattered heart. I have never managed to experience a love relationship beyond its terrible two's, and although there has only been one incident of such magnified violence, all my relationships have ended on less-than-ideal terms.

"It is important for you to get to know a person before making the steps to move in with them, mtshana, and that can take up to three years." Uncle JS's advice makes me think long and hard. My track record shows that I usually move in with a lover within two weeks of meeting them.

I have similar conversations with my friend Lethu, who is there for me day and night as I battle through the loneliness that comes with self-reflection and heartbreak. One Saturday morning, waking up alone in my bed, as I lift my heavy head from my pillow, wondering how I will make it through the silence of another weekend of being single, I receive a WhatsApp voice note from Lethu.

Love awaits your arrival like a woman with child, pregnant with a new life that will magically find its way into the dying parts of you.

You will be born again in love and you will soon rediscover the world with a new freedom.

Like a baby finding her feet, you will come to know that falling when you try is not registered as a fail; it is as good and as great as a gigantic step forward.

When you awake in the warmth of love's arms, that strange familiarity you will feel will serve to affirm that you have arrived where you were long anticipated.

You will be born again in love and all the wounds of past hurts that once stained your heart will be licked away.

Your pain will no longer be a point of reference to be used as an excuse to hide yourself from love.

You will come to acknowledge every thorn you have ever laid your foot on, every frog you have ever kissed and every tear you have ever tasted as nothing new to a baby who had a curiosity to feed.

Although she has not written the poem specifically for me, her words come at exactly the right time, when I have reached rock bottom, the very pit of my soul, when all the pain I have endured has finally made me open and able to listen. I replay the voice note repeatedly, and once I have transcribed it onto paper I begin absorbing the words and applying them to my life. Every painful step I have walked has been part of my journey to find the love of self.

Instead of seeing myself as a victim and blaming the people who have hurt me, I now see the huge amount of pain and damage I have caused in the lives of others. I realise how I have sabotaged my own progress, how I've neglected the advice of my doctors who warned me time and time again not to indulge recklessly in alcohol. I confront how great a role alcohol has played in the breakdown of my relationships, how I have used it to numb the pain of abandonment, hoping to fill a void when things go wrong in the matters of the heart.

I go back to my trusted friend Google and search: how to curb the urge to drink when dealing with depression and anger. I come across Alcoholics Anonymous (AA), an international twelve-step fellowship that helps people become and stay sober. There are plenty of meetings all over Cape Town. My initial reaction is defence and denial: there is no way I am an alcoholic. I try to convince myself that I function very well on a daily basis and, despite my financial problems, I am able to sustain my life without seeking assistance from anyone.

Still resistant, I reluctantly scan information on the AA home page. I decide that the only way to fully gauge what goes on in these meetings and whether I fit the alcoholic profile or not is to attend one of the get-togethers.

I locate a meeting in the Milnerton Methodist church not too far from where I live and attend my first meeting towards the end of March 2015. As I walk into the church hall, with about thirty men and women of different ages and races, I am reminded of Uncle JS's words: "The only shame is having shame when you know you need help."

An elderly white lady welcomes me and invites me to sit next to her in the circle of chairs. I am silent throughout the first meeting, observing each person as they introduce themselves as an alcoholic. I listen to tale after tale about people who have lost their children, their families, their homes to alcohol. How what began as a social hobby has become a nightmare, often driving the alcoholic to the brink of suicide. Most of the 'confessions' are about the need to drink and the inability to stay sober, even for an hour a day. I leave the meeting torn. I am even more uncertain about whether I should self-diagnose as an alcoholic or not. What I do know is that I feel shame.

I will not seek counsel from Uncle JS on this one. This is something I need to do on my own. I begin weaning myself from the drink and find ways to fill my days. I continue going to meetings if only to hear what could lie in store for me if I do not pull myself towards myself. I am inspired by the courage of these people to confront their demons and I'm determined to learn from their mistakes. Through listening, I learn how to desist the urge to turn to what has become my crutch.

Two months later I feel I have gained the insight I need to get my life back on track and stop attending AA meetings. I now drink only to unwind, a glass of wine here and there, and have long since parted ways with my once trusted confidant, Smirnoff 1818. But I have learned a lot about seeing myself clearly without the blinkers of blame and denial. And when I accept my part in my own downfall, I experience an unexpected lightening of my soul.

THIRTY-TWO

Loving Landa

By the time 2016 rolls in I am inspired to fully immerse myself into Operation Return to Landa: drawing up a plan to figure out the real purpose of my life.

I fully commit to continue to declutter my mind of all the cruel and hateful thoughts I have about myself, to unlearn everything I have been conditioned to believe. I know I have to empty my mind so that I can fill it with purpose and self-love, and since relationships are the place where I struggle most, I take Uncle JS's advice and decide to stay away from all romantic relationships, and work instead on finding healthier ways to bolster myself.

I come to realise, too, that it's not only alcohol I've been using to numb myself; comfort eating has also been my fix. The craving, lust even, for KFC, McDonald's, deep-fried snoek and slap chips has me weighing a whopping 108 kilograms. I have truly let myself go. Between drinking and over-eating, combined with the unmonitored testosterone injections, I resemble an inflated balloon. So I swallow my pride, join the Century City Athletics Club and am soon a regular at the Saturday-morning 10-kilometre races across Cape Town. And the more I run, the more I peel away the layers of shame and unwanted body fat. When I'm out on the road, the tar beneath my feet, I connect with my mind as it drifts into worlds undiscovered and find myself plotting out my new life.

My vitals soon begin to improve and my life-threatening high blood pressure, which I have chosen to ignore, now becomes less of an issue. I put my dream for phalloplasty surgery on hold. Although this will complete the work that has already begun to fully align my genitals with my self, I need to address my immediate financial commitments so that I can pay off the debts that I've accumulated over the past two years. Besides, I want to save up for further surgical interventions beyond the borders of this country where more specialised care is available with amazing outcomes. One quote – from the London Andrology Centre – came in at £62 000 for the series of surgeries that will be required.

By the time I turn thirty-five and travel to Mthatha for a traditional thanksgiving ceremony, I am down to 85 kilograms. Of course, there are those gossipers who are convinced I have contracted some incurable disease and am dying. This only inspires me to keep focused on my plans to develop and improve myself. When I leave, I realise I have come a long way by not allowing the cruelty of others to derail me.

The year 2016 continues to see me shifting the limitations I've previously imposed on my life. I now thrive with every step I walk or run. By training harder, I manage to complete the Two Oceans 21-kilometre Half Marathon as well as the Sanlam Cape Town 42-kilometre full marathon.

With all these changes, it now becomes clear that I need to leave the comfort of the nest that is my day job, where I've been employed for the past eighteen months as assistant director with Western Cape Government Health Department. I have got to a point where I can perform my duties with my eyes closed – I need a challenge that will force me to dream bigger.

I resign in August and spend the next two months in meditation. I split my life into four sections: the child who was loved until the age of eleven, the teen who was violently abused, the adult who carried the wounds, and the new self who is now working towards transformative love for the self and others. For the first time, I truly see how selfish I have become, trapped in my own pain and self-pity. So I decide to invest some of my time in the service of others, to help those who need someone in their corner, to believe that their lives matter and that they are capable of much more than what the world has thrown at them. So I sign up with SAYes youth mentoring and became part of a pool of mentors who provide guidance, advocacy and support to youth in state facilities. The weekly engagements with my mentees give me a new sense of purpose and help me to regain the focus and confidence I lost all those years ago.

With the gifts one gets from giving back, I experience a new kind of fullness for the first time in my life. I decide I want to focus more on the transgender advocacy space, and in September of 2016, I register an independent consultancy, Landa Mabenge Consulting, with the primary purpose of creating educational awareness and linkages to healthcare for young people at university level who identify as transgender.

It dawns on me more urgently than ever that I am here to serve a very specific purpose, and though my gender identity is not unique in the grander scheme of things, the intricacies of my particular journey are special and unique to me. I embrace my newfound purpose: I am here to create an arena in which to inspire others who struggle, like I once did, to align their existence to their core.

Without the restrictions of a day job, I now immerse myself in historical research and unearth a wealth of literature from as far back as the early seventeenth century, where different nations and tribes, especially among the Native American and African people, recognised the fluidity and variance of gender, in particular those they deemed mediums between the two conventions of male and female. I am fascinated to discover that the decline of recognition and respect for gender-variant people, who were often regarded as mystics and gate keepers between the two worlds, was largely inspired by the onslaught of colonialism, with its violent male heteronormative patriarchal practices. I am particularly impressed by two authors – Sobonfu Somé and Malidoma Patrice Somé – from Burkina Faso, who inspire me to explore the intimate connection between spirituality, gender and relationships in a traditional African context.

When the calendar ticks over to January 2017 I am amazed

at how much has changed in my life within the short space of a year, by simply changing the thoughts I have about myself. Now I decide to throw all caution to the wind and audition for The Philharmonia Choir of Cape Town. Singing has been a childhood passion but I last sang in a choir in Grade 10. The Mother forced me to give it up back then, complaining that the practice times were an inconvenience.

When I walk into Westerford High School one morning to audition with the Director of the Choir, Richard Haigh, I know I have but one shot, especially given the fact that I can no longer read music. So it is that I am overjoyed to be accepted into the choir and am allowed a shot as Tenor 2. From First Soprano when I was in Grade 10 to Tenor 2, oh how things have changed. In March, I realise a lifelong dream and sing in the chorus of Handel's *Messiah*, accompanied by the Cape Town Philharmonic Orchestra. With the aid of a training CD, I have managed to learn the tenor part in two weeks. Like my marathon running, this proves to me once again that I can achieve anything I set my mind to.

While my life is blossoming in new directions, there is the inevitable fall-out with some of my siblings in my immediate family. By concentrating on me, it's been easier to remove myself from the shackles of obligations I once had. The siblings I once was trained to serve now accuse me of being selfish. But this time I manage to keep my boundaries and accept that, just like me, they are victims of a system designed and executed to create an imbalance and hierarchy among children who came from the same womb.

I continue immersing myself in motivational videos that all have a common message: in order to truly engage in life and be of service to others, I must first fix up myself. I can no longer afford to put Landa second.

A month after my Handel's *Messiah* singing debut, I receive a letter confirming that I have been selected for the 2017 Mandela Washington Fellowship, out of 64 000 applicants across the African continent. I will be part of a contingent of a thousand young African leaders, jetting off to the United States of America for six weeks between June and August 2017.

I can barely contain myself as I read how I have been chosen to hone my civic leadership abilities to impact the work I do through my transgender consultancy. Oh, how the winds have changed in my favour. The universe has given me a huge and mighty sign that there are untold possibilities for a person who was denied the very basics in terms of provision and care as a child. It is mind-blowing affirmation of how much can be achieved through concerted hard work and self-healing.

A few days later I attend the launch of *Being Chris Hani's Daughter* co-written by Lindiwe Hani and her publisher Melinda Ferguson. Little do I know how significant this event will be in the bigger picture of my healing and life's purpose.

I am brimming with joy, still on a high from my US letter when I arrive at The Book Lounge in Cape Town's CBD.

I watch Lindiwe walk into the venue, accompanied by her publisher, Melinda; I have never heard of Melinda, but immediately notice her undeniable presence. Her ruby-coloured hair flows as she saunters around the tightly packed venue, acting as a medium between Lindi and her many guests.

I am transfixed by the dialogue between the two as Lindi talks about her life as the daughter of one of South Africa's greatest fallen heroes. She openly unpacks her addictions, the sorrows of losing her father so violently and of her journey of recovery, inspiring her to invest in a new life based on taking it one day at a time. By the time the evening comes to a close, I cannot contain my tears. The night has profoundly affected me. I leave with a deep desire to write my own story.

I drive home in silence, knowing that it is time to once again look at my toxic self and peel back the scab of continued healing. In reality, I know I still have a long journey to travel.

I think of the AA meetings I have attended, trying to measure the degree of alcoholism I have diagnosed for myself. Although I know that I have grossly abused liquor and used it as a crutch, what I have really been evading is the mammoth evil that is anger. As I drive into the night, I wonder whether I will ever cross paths with Melinda again. I have a deep desire to find a way to connect with her, to pitch her the idea for my book. I pray to the stars above and surrender my dream to the great universe and for my ancestors to guide it, whatever the outcome will be.

The day 15 June arrives, my bags are packed and I am ready to board my flight to the US. This is the first time I'll be travelling outside of South Africa. I arrive at Cape Town International Airport, escorted by my girlfriend Yonga Jizana, whom I have been living with for just over six months. We have known each other for more than a decade and she understands just how amazing this opportunity is for me.

After an emotional goodbye, I board a KLM flight destined for Charlottesville, Virginia. As the plane takes off and soars into the night skies I am reminded of the dark days of childhood and university, where I would scramble for food or rely on friends for my meals. How far I have come!

After hours of delays at customs in Atlanta, I finally arrive at the small airport in Charlottesville on the evening of 16 June 2017. I am met by a warm contingent of staff from the Presidential Precinct, a non-profit organisation affiliated to the University of Virginia, The College of William and Mary and the Foundations of America's Founding Fathers: Thomas Jefferson, James Madison and James Munroe, headed by Director of Programs Nancy Hopkins.

I spend the next six weeks interacting and learning from other fellows while lapping up life-enhancing lectures. By the time the entire cohort of a thousand fellows descends on Washington DC for a three-day summit to conclude our experience in the States, I am both exhausted and exhilarated. I have grown in unimaginable ways and fired up to inject my consultancy with service offerings inspired by the mountains of knowledge I have gleaned from the various leaders in academia, business and politics.

My feathers are further fluffed when, while still in the US, I am granted a scholarship to attend the inaugural Botswana Dialogue on Science, Spirituality and Humanity with His Holiness, the fourteenth Dalai Lama, whose book *The Art of Happiness* served as a compass when I was trying to pick up the pieces of my shattered life. I am once again amazed at how the universe is providing me with tools to support my new-found purpose on this earth.

Two weeks after returning from the US, in August 2017, I travel to Botswana in great spirits, eager to touch the hem of the garment of the man whose wisdom has inspired me to return to humanity. When his entourage informs us that His Holiness will be unable to attend due to ill-health, although disappointed, I immerse myself in the many conversations hosted by the Mind and Life institute, soaking in as much as I can. I am in awe of the array of speakers from different walks of life who share inspiring and thought-provoking perspectives, interweaving the areas of spirit, science and humanity. Due to His Holiness's absence, I am granted, as part of a youth panel, an impromptu opportunity to make a presentation on the work that I do.

As I take to the podium, I feel humbled to be of service and regarded as relevant enough to speak at an event where so many have gathered to hear one of the most compassionate world leaders in history, a man who has ignited the flame of healing and compassion in my life and helped me to impart that to others.

It is not so much about the platform or having a chance to speak, but when I think of where I have come from, it is evident to me that the invisible hand of the universe is guiding and blessing me. I am deeply convinced that in life there is no such thing as a coincidence. It feels like every single step of my journey has been mapped out long before I came into being. The lesson I leave Botswana with stays with me long after the event: what first appears to be a disappointment or a curse can turn into an enormous blessing. And that is the art of happiness.

Afterword

I have spent much of my life adrift in hollow silos, a bee whirling around inside an empty can. I have existed in the "dreams" hidden behind the false picket fences of suburbia, where I was trained to believe that my footprint on earth was tied to inevitable failure. I have salvaged the scraps intended for dogs driven by pangs of hunger. I have lived a directionless, hungover life, not knowing or understanding what the dynamics of my biological constructs would yield, in a world that has outright rejected the beauty of the spectrum that lies between the indoctrinated conventions of what gender and sexuality ought to look like.

But it is along the modest dusty streets of my home in Ncambedlana, Mthatha, that I truly found myself. It is within the folds of the love I received there that I have learned to embrace my inner butterfly – to see, change and finally accept myself for who I truly am. It is within the warmth of my early childhood home, to which I returned in 2001, where I found the tools I needed to piece myself back together, and discover the passions that always resonated within my soul.

I sometimes wonder how, as a spirit, I made the decision to choose The Parents I landed up with. I reflect on their often inexplicable efforts to suppress and break me, and I wonder if my deity had specific intentions when he/she/it placed me with them.

I unpack the brutalities I have faced, and though during dark and trying times I never imagined I would be where I currently am, I am always inspired by the underlying pulse of love that has always reverberated in my life. All these years later, I am often reminded of my History teacher Wendy Rossouw, who always inspired me to give my best in her class by drumming the words of Celine Dion into my head, "It's all coming back to me now."

Perhaps, as a spirit, I did choose my hosts in flesh. Perhaps I identified those who needed the most healing and allowed myself to go through their pain and my own early on in life, so that I could know better and, in knowing, do better. Perhaps as a spirit I chose my body, my mother, my father, and did so with the determination that I would emerge the teacher that I am. Along the way I have learned to embrace humility, and it is my hope that, in doing so, I will impart that to humanity.

But humility is a work in progress and there are times when I need to work on practising tolerance. Whenever individuals question my 'genitals' I am reminded of how blinkered and obsessed with labels we humans are. Whatever lies between my legs, whether I sit or stand when I pee, my genitals are what they are and they serve their purpose. Whatever the shape, size or name of them, and whether I have chosen to surgically align my body to my identity or not, I remain the man I have always been.

But perhaps my greatest lesson, through all the pain, self-loathing and hardships, is being able to embrace the beauty of individuality and the importance of identity and self-love. Whatever decisions I have made regarding my body have been mine to make. I have been met with admiration by some and outright rejection by others, and still I remain, me, Landa. The journey continues, as life does, with all its ups and downs and ebbs and flows – the tapestry part-woven and my purpose an ever-filling well of enlightenment.

Acknowledgements

Writing this book has been tougher than I had imagined it would be. I reflect with gratitude on all the people and spirits that have journeyed with me:

To my publisher Melinda Ferguson and her publishing imprint MFBooks Joburg. Thank you for having me at hello and for immersing yourself into the birthing of *Becoming Him*. I am grateful for the writing workshops I attended at your home, the late nights and early mornings, and the endless hours you have invested into this book. I reflect on the past couple of months and whenever I count my blessings, I count you twice.

Thank you to the team at Jacana Media, especially Bridget Impey, who has been a guiding compass at all times.

To Birgit Schreiber. Thank you for saving my life.

To Yonga Jizana, the love of my life. Thank you for your seamless patience throughout the writing of this book. You saw me battle with the darkness at times and kept reminding me to focus on the light. Thank you lover yam.

To the clinical team at the Transgender Clinic at Groote Schuur Hospital, the Triangle Project and the brothers who walked this journey with me during my early days (Robert, Tebogo and Yoli). Thank you for the milestones you have helped me achieve.

To the friends I met and got to know during my time in Port

Elizabeth, especially Vuyo Matana (Vee) and Dianne Jopson. You made my transition from love to rejection a bit bearable. Thank you.

A very special thank you to the friends who tried so selflessly to shield me from myself and my darkness at the University of Cape Town (UCT). The pages in this book would never be enough to detail the path we walked together. Thank you to all of you.

Thank you to the friends I made during my working career. Though there are too many to mention, I especially thank Nurahn and Shamieg Ryklief, Wayne, Bronwyn and Ethan Petersen, Bulelwa Mshudulu, Nolo Malothane and my dream team Mincili Mandindi, Loyiso Mfunda, Onkgopotse Moahloli, Josiah Sinankwa and Vuyokazi Renqe. I am grateful for your continued presence and friendship.

To my day ones: Lelethu Mahambehlala (Lethu) and Thandiwe Klaas (Thandi). I choose you every single day. Thank you for loving me the way you do.

Thank you to the many friends who have at any given point been pillars of sanity in my life. A special thank you to Bandisiwe Cabangana-Mnyanda, Vuyokazi Ntshinga (Vo), Lwazikazi Gqoli and Botho Montshiwa.

Thank you to Tabisa (Tash) and Lubambo Sithole and their children for always making time for me and my journey.

A big thank you to the 2017 Mandela Washington cohort of Fellows, especially my little Presidential Precinct Family. You will never know just how grateful I am to be counted as part of such a diverse and progressive group of young leaders.

To all the Ncambedlana families who have been integral to my growth during my early childhood years and later when I returned home to Mthatha. A special thank you to the Jizana, Noah, Yako, Jele, Madala, Luthi, Ntloko, Tshandu, Mpahlwa, Stofile, Raziya, Socikwa, Nondwane, Nyimbana, Mda, Menye and Gwiliza families. I would not have any other community to call my own.

To my family. To my grandparents John and Olga Danana (Mzalwane and Miss K). Thank you for giving birth to me through your daughter. To uncle John Sembie Danana, his wife and children, to aunt Patiswa Pumla Danana and her beautiful sons, to my uncles Viwe Songo Danana and Feza Danana and my aunts Liziwe Matoti and Cikizwa Danana. Words could never quantify how grateful I am to have all of you as my home.

To my extended family, cousins and my half siblings Linda Ndzamela and Loyiso Jekubeni and their children. Thank you.

To my brother Mncedi Mabenge. We made it my guy. I love you.

Finally, to the woman who cradled me in her arms when I was a day old. To the one who crossed the Kei bridge with me when I was two days old. To the mother who sacrificed her life and made sure that I mattered. To the heart that continues to resonate within the folds of my being. To my everything. To Nomha Vuyelwa Danana, my Ma. Thank you for loving me so selflessly without expectation. Thank you for giving me the best years of my childhood and the best of you. I will always love you.